Teams for a New Generation

A Facilitator's Field Guide

GREG ROBINSON AND MARK ROSE

authorHOUSE®

AuthorHouse™
1663 Liberty Drive, Suite 200
Bloomington, IN 47403
www.authorhouse.com
Phone: 1-800-839-8640

©2007 Greg Robinson and Mark Rose. All rights reserved.

No part of this book may be reproduced, stored in a retrieval system, or transmitted by any means without the written permission of the author.

First published by AuthorHouse 10/9/2007

ISBN: 978-1-4343-2411-5 (e)
ISBN: 978-1-4343-2410-8 (sc)

Library of Congress Control Number: 2007906394

Printed in the United States of America
Bloomington, Indiana

This book is printed on acid-free paper.

Table of Contents

Introduction vii

Chapter 1 1
The Facilitator's Greatest Gift

Chapter 2 5
Creating a Common Language – *Collective Learning*

Chapter 3 11
Indicators of Learning

Chapter 4 17
The Dynamics of Collective Learning

Chapter 5 29
Critical Opportunities for Facilitators

Chapter 6 41
Relational Awareness

Chapter 7 49
Personal Awareness

Chapter 8 59
Organizational Awareness

Chapter 9 67
Signs of Hidden Assumptions

Chapter 10 77
The Possibilities of Teams That Learn Collectively

Tools 81

Activities for Developing New Generation Teams 123

Notes 154

Bibliography 157

About the Authors 161

Introduction

"Which questions guide our lives? Which questions do we make our own? Which questions deserve our undivided attention and full personal commitment? Finding the right questions is as crucial as finding the right answers."
Henri Nouwen - <u>The Way of the Heart</u>

I am an experiential facilitator and consultant by trade. Experiential means that I make shared experiences the launching point for learning and encourage intentional reflection on those experiences to promote learning. Several years ago, I began to notice in my work with groups that although I was facilitating some interesting conversations that resulted in some change, there seemed to be little lasting effect.

As a facilitator, I find that one of my favorite tools is a challenge course. A challenge course is a series of physical and mental challenges that require teamwork to successfully complete them. I remember watching a group struggle on a particular element. After the group completed the task, we gathered to reflect on what had happened. Some very good learning (I use that word guardedly) occurred. The group members were able to identify what they did and the results of their behavior. They were even able to describe other ways of behaving that would yield more desirable results. We then walked fifty feet to one side and started the next element. The group members behaved as if the previous discussion had never happened and were unable to apply what they had learned to this element. This experience made me consider why the discussions and experiences had so little lasting effect on the participants. As I took a more inclusive look at all the learning and change activity going on around me, I realized that getting people to change their actions and their words did not necessarily mean you were changing *them*. Looking back, I now know I was helping groups to rearrange the surface, but nothing had really changed deep within them. For real change, people must change their perceptions of themselves and their world. Here is an early example in my life when my paradigms shifted.

When I was young, maybe six or seven years old, I was sitting in my living room on Christmas Eve. My heart thrilled with the anticipation of all I would get the following morning. As I was entranced by my childish greed, an idea suddenly crashed into my consciousness. I not only could receive gifts at Christmas; I could also give them. I jumped up and ran into my bedroom in a real panic. I only had a few hours, no money and no ideas. That intrusive thought forever changed the way I looked at Christmas, or for that matter, the way I looked at life. That thought changed the way I perceived my family, my world and myself. This was one of those moments when my paradigms shifted.

Realizing that I was only helping groups rearrange the surface was another paradigm shift similar to the Christmas story that resulted, for me, in a new way of thinking about group work. I had to begin asking a different set of questions. I had been ignoring some very important dimensions of the people with whom I was working. I had been reflecting only on the most visible dimension—behavior. However, somewhere just out of sight, something existed that drove the behavior. Since that discovery, I have worked at developing skills, attitudes and tools to work with the other dimensions of human activity. Emotions and beliefs are crucial to any successful learning. The problem is, they are often unnoticed and, thus, control behavior from the shadows.

This book is a compilation of what I have learned. At its core, this book focuses on how a facilitator can help groups, and the individuals in those groups, to slow down their emotional and belief processes to create opportunities to choose responses, rather than being completely reactive. The purpose of the facilitator's effort is to move experiential learning beyond the traditional notion of teambuilding. Teambuilding has become a catchall phrase for helping group members become more comfortable with one another and develop trust. I think that to unlock the power of these experiential tools, facilitators must think about developing meta-skills. Using experiential learning to develop the attitudes and skills to continually learn provides a real hope for creating fundamental change in the way people and groups interact.

Greg Robinson

Note to the reader:

Throughout this book we refer to a facilitator with masculine and feminine pronouns (he and she). An effective facilitator is one who helps a group and it does not matter their gender. We will also refer to Greg and Mark interchangeably in the first and third person voice. This is meant to maintain efficiency and clarity throughout the book and provide an easier read. Finally, since this is meant to be a Field Guide, we have intentionally widened the outside margins for you to make notes. We hope you find this guide practical and that it becomes a resource for you to use again and again.

Chapter 1
The Facilitator's Greatest Gift

"When you learn how to die, you learn how to live."
Mitch Albom - <u>Tuesdays with Morrie</u>

Occasionally, a person may come across a truth so important that it is almost overlooked because it comes in such a simple package. We firmly believe that the most important tool a facilitator brings to a group is himself or herself. Consequently, what can cause the greatest limitation to a developing team is also the facilitator. This chapter will be a collection of thoughts concerning attitudes, beliefs, values and assumptions we find critical to being a good facilitator. Some will seem obvious; others may leave you scratching your head. Regardless, basic facilitation is about letting go.

Here is a quote that has really helped us understand what a facilitator needs to do if groups are going to learn. We have adapted it somewhat, but have not quenched its spirit:

> Hospitality, therefore, means primarily the creating of a free space where the team member can enter and become a friend instead of an enemy. Hospitality is not to change people, but to offer them space where change can take place. It is not to bring men and women over to our side, but to

offer freedom not disturbed by dividing lines. It is not to lead our teammates into a corner where there are no alternatives left, but to open a wide spectrum of options for choice and commitment. It is not an educated intimidation with good books, good stories, and good works, but the liberation of fearful hearts so that words can find roots and bear ample fruit. It is not a method of making . . . our way into the criteria of happiness, but the opening of an opportunity to others to find their own way.[1]

Experiential facilitation often carries the mystique, or stigma, depending on one's perspective, of being too touchy-feely. We hope the negative connotations can be suspended because hospitality is a great place to start our discussion.

Hospitality, making a safe place where others can be honest with themselves and one another, is not a simple task. It requires some extraordinary things of the facilitator who would seek to create such a place. To begin, hospitality requires that the facilitator has taken an honest look inward. The hospitable facilitator is aware of his own fears, preferences, pressure points and gifts. Our basic premise is that awareness combined with courage creates choice. Because a facilitator knows himself or herself better and exercises his or her choice, a facilitator develops the inner freedom so very necessary to be a good host to groups. The facilitator's first responsibility is to let go of those fears that would hinder the team's development. The facilitator is there for the group, and not vice versa. A good facilitator has other places from which to draw support, value and a sense of meaning. If the facilitator expects to obtain these things from the group, he will be of little value to the team and will avoid those things that cause discomfort, which are the very things that the team most needs help in recognizing. What should be happening is that the facilitator is able to absorb some of the team's anxiety and communicate a commitment to the process. This

> **The facilitator's first responsibility is to let go of those fears that would hinder the team's development. The facilitator is there for the group, and not vice versa.**

vicarious confidence will allow the team to take the all-important first steps toward honest, open communication.

There are some other important values the hospitable facilitator will need. She must value truth over comfort. Too often, mistakes are hidden and potential learning is lost when individuals cannot tolerate the discomfort of being wrong long enough to learn from their mistakes. Another way truth over comfort gets played out is in the pull of the system to stay the same. Any time a person seeks truth over comfort, that person will be perceived as a threat to others around the individual. Consequently, those people who make up the various systems (co-workers, family members or friends) will try, either through seduction or sabotage, to get the person hooked back into being dependent on the system. It is often easier to just go along than to do the right thing.

The facilitator must believe that participants are more than their behavior. People are never as good as their best efforts and never as bad as their worst deeds. Letting go of certainty includes believing there is more to the situation than what can be perceived by the senses. A facilitator must learn to recognize defensive scripts when she sees one. If a facilitator is to foster deep learning in groups, she will undoubtedly see participants at their worst. If you can look past the mess to see what might be, you will extend a real sense of safety to the group.

There was a time in Greg's life when he was quite concerned with getting people to ask the right questions. In his arrogance and concern (a very strange partnership), he believed the questions people were trying to ask would never yield the answers they truly wanted to hear. To be fair, Greg was not playing Monday-morning quarterback with other people's lives. He was asking himself some very different questions. His friend and mentor gave him one of the greatest gifts Greg has ever received. This friend explained it was not Greg's responsibility to get anyone to ask the right kinds of questions. All Greg had to do was to ask the right kinds of questions of himself, in their presence. That would be enough to make a difference. The result for Greg was a real sense of relief. No longer would he have to find ways to make people learn and grow. Being curious would draw others into his curiosity, and he could influence them, quite unintentionally.

There is a technique for helping people get over a low, challenge course element called the Team Wall that is a living metaphor for this. The Team Wall is a smooth-faced, fourteen-foot wall that a team must get the entire group over without the aid of any equipment. As you can imagine, pulling people over such an obstacle is no easy task. Sometimes a group will discover that if the people at the top of the wall take the climber by the hand and extend their arms away from the wall, the climber can just walk up the wall, using friction to move. This technique contains the greatest risk for an uncontrolled fall. However, done correctly, the technique places minimal stress on any one person. Why? Because this technique requires everyone do just his or her part, and no more. If the helpers at the top panic and pull the climber close to the wall in an attempt to regain control, they disable the climber from helping. The climber becomes dead weight, and the burden becomes tremendous. Ultimately, what we want to illustrate is that if a facilitator can learn to let go of control and predictability, he will be able to help team members hold onto one another through those difficult times when trust is being established and honesty is being promoted.

Conclusion

All the tools and processes that follow are first meant to be practiced by the facilitator personally. Only then will a facilitator become familiar enough with them to be able to wield them in an atmosphere of safety for others. Two primary areas of focus are Collective Learning and Process Facilitation. Collective Learning will be discussed in the next four chapters, and Process Facilitation will be discussed in Chapter 6.

Chapter 2
Creating a Common Language – Collective Learning

"Grasp the subject, the words will follow."
Cato the Elder, *Roman orator and politician*

Collective Learning is a discipline. It often results in closeness and cohesion, but Collective Learning is not dependent on warm feelings. Groups that embody Collective Learning are responsible for their own choices and, as a result, are able to maintain and renew their groups when needed. These groups are not only aware of their assumptions, values and beliefs; the groups challenge their values and assumptions to ensure they are operating with a mindset that represents truth.

Margaret Wheatley and Myron Kellner-Rogers outline a change process that puts what we are trying to say another way. They suggest that change begins with a system noticing something and allowing itself to be disturbed by this. As this something is circulated, it grows and changes through multiple interpretations. Ultimately, the system is forced to let go of past beliefs as it becomes more aware of a new reality. In the end, "it [the system] re-creates itself around new understandings of what is real and what's important. It becomes different because it understands the world differently."[1] Teams that can practice Collective Learning can enter this process intentionally. Being intentional grows from an inner motivation. It may be in response to external stimuli, but being intentional does not require external force to be the catalyst for learning. There is a need for this new way of thinking about teams. We will begin the discussion of this new mindset by focusing on three fundamental polarities that are inherent in group dynamics.

A polarity is a pair of seemingly opposite ideas that over time are both required if success or health is to be maintained.[2] There is always a tension between the two poles that will never go away. Polarities are not problems to be solved but require constant, ongoing attention for them to be managed. Everyone who is reading this page is a master of managing polarities. We know this because you have been managing a critical polarity since you were born. Try an experiment for a moment. On the count of three, make a simple choice between inhaling or exhaling. Once you make the choice, hold it until indicated otherwise. Okay, one, two, three—choose. Whatever your choice, initially there is complete assurance that it was absolutely the right choice. Your lungs felt relief as oxygen poured in or carbon dioxide rushed out. However, about now you are starting to experience the limitation of your choice. Consequently, the exact opposite of your choice seems more right now. Okay, breathe normally. Inhaling and exhaling is a fundamental polarity of life. You cannot have one without the other. Trying to live with one and not the other seems ridiculous. Yet, when it comes to teams, we are constantly trying to live at one end of three fundamental polarities. If we can accept these three polarities, we will be on the path to a new way of thinking about team dynamics. Those polarities are 1) the individual vs. the team, 2) action vs. reflection and 3) stability vs. change.

The Individual vs. the Team

When teams are forming or attempting to improve their effectiveness, there tends to be a focus on the team end of this polarity. Things that are of concern are cohesion, boundaries, collective identity and shared vision. There is a priority placed on fitting in and getting along. Collective Learning suggests this is only half the answer.

By nature, when someone emphasizes one end of a polarity to the exclusion of the other end, over time there will be a significant loss of effectiveness. Too often, individuals want to view this struggle as an either/or choice. Do not be forced into trying to choose between the two ends of this continuum. Truth is closer to the center. Focusing on the team to the exclusion of the individual results in groupthink, mediocrity and a loss of accountability. Focusing on the individual to the exclusion of the team results in chaos, anarchy and dissent. A strong team must have both. To be a strong team, the team members must be strong individuals. On the other hand, the only thing that will allow individuals the freedom to examine themselves is a strong supportive community. The burden of self-discovery is too heavy to bear alone. Consequently, when we begin to explore the learning wheel model of Collective Learning in Chapter 4, the facilitator should apply the principles to the individuals and the group as a whole.

The important point of this discussion is that in Collective Learning the team improves by helping individuals change themselves rather than changing each other. The individuals who make up the team must become aware of the assumptions they make, the choices they enact and the behavior they exhibit. Only then will they be able to take responsibility for themselves and thus participate more freely in the life of the team. This should be balanced with a focus on shared vision and purpose, an awareness of the collective assumptions being made and the shared expectations of the team.

> *The individuals who make up the team must become aware of the assumptions they make, the choices they enact and the behavior they exhibit.*

Action vs. Reflection

A second polarity facilitators should consider is action versus reflection. When action is primary to the exclusion of reflection, the result is repeated mistakes, hasty decisions and rework. Consequently, when reflection is emphasized to the exclusion of action, the result is analysis paralysis and good intentions but no results. Just as in all polarities, there must be a balance of both.

Collective Learning focuses on slowing down enough to take more considered action. Reflection is the beginning and end of good group dynamics. Stepping back to plan and check the shared understanding of the objectives is the first step of reflection. The best teams then close the circle by reflecting on their shared experience to capture the lessons they've learned. In addition, collective reflection is the foundation of building a culture that will support collaboration.

When teaching teams the foundations of group dynamics, helping them develop patience for reflection is important. Most teams will err on the action side, although we have often experienced teams that want to talk and discuss but not take action. When that logjam is reached, remind the team members that the only way they will ever know if they are right is to take the first step.

Change vs. Stability

This third polarity suggests that healthy teams require stability and the ability to continue to change and adapt. In our opinion, most of the traditional information about teams reinforces the stability end of the polarity. Roles, norms, objectives, processes and rules of behavior are constructs that make the relationships in teams clear. Such constructs provide boundaries around what is expected and acceptable behavior within a team. The benefit they provide is that they bring clarity to the messiness of the human relationships within a team. Done well, stability forces eliminate unnecessary anxiety that is created by lack of direction and role confusion. The stability constructs provide threshold conditions for higher-order team activity. However, focusing on the stability pole to the exclusion of the change pole results in rigidity. Collaboration (higher-order team activity) cannot be mandated or regulated. It can only be facilitated.

Such a facilitator will need to struggle with the idea that stability requires uncertainty. Although it may seem absurd on the surface, science is discovering that what allows the material world to remain the same is things are always changing. Our bodies are in constant motion of change. Did you know that our skin is totally new every four weeks, our livers every six weeks and even our brains are new every twelve months?[2] Change is intimidating because it requires us to let go of certainty. Control is but an illusion. Too often, facilitators struggle to maintain control of the group. Some ways to know if you are a facilitator who hangs onto the illusion or is comfortable with uncertainty is to notice how you respond to situations where the unexpected pops up. What happens if the group wants to discuss something other than what you, the facilitator, think is important? If that situation sends your heart right into your throat, you are hanging on too tightly. To really let go and be okay with uncertainty, the facilitator must have a strongly rooted identity. This kind of facilitator is assured of his or her importance and value regardless of how well the team does. This kind of letting go allows the facilitator to be an 'objective' observer. No one is truly objective. Everyone views the world with some bias. The closest we can get is to have an emotional distance from the group's performance. This means the facilitator does not have the emotional baggage and investment that the team has.

Conclusion

It is important to realize that the mistake that is often made with teams is to think that by establishing stability, a team can fix its problems. Too often, what is really called for is an increased ability for the team and the individual members to change and adapt. You cannot fix dynamic problems with static solutions. What is called for is to understand the change pole and help team members develop the ability to continue to learn from and with each other.

Chapter 3
Indicators of Learning

"What is important is to keep learning, to enjoy challenge, and to tolerate ambiguity. In the end there are no certain answers."
                                    Martina Horner, *President of Radcliffe College*

Healthy teams continue to grow, mature and change over time. To us, the word *learning* captures this process. Although we could substitute the word change for learning, we like learning for a couple of reasons. First, learning says that this activity is purposeful and intentional. We all change over time, but we do not all pay attention to how we change or what changes are occurring. Learning, on the other hand, speaks to a process that a person participates in for a reason and is seeking some result. Likewise, teams that continue to grow in their effectiveness will purposefully continue to learn from and with all team members. In line with the first reason, learning results in individuals and teams making meaning of their experiences. Not only is learning an intentional activity but, when mastered, allows teams and individuals within those teams to repeat their success when needed. Many teams have success, but not many teams know why they were successful, or are able to replicate the success in different settings.

A facilitator knows teams are learning when . . .
- There is an increased *awareness of assumptions* and mental models.

- There is an increase in individuals and the group's ability to *manage differences*.
- There is an *expanded perspective*.

Awareness of Assumptions

When we begin to think about the desired outcomes of change, the focus is generally on some behavior or action. Generally, when people pursue change, they want to do something different in the end. We agree that real change will affect the way we act, work and interact with others. In other words, our behavior will change. However, when change agents try to alter behavior first and exclusively, the sustainability of that change is limited. The reason is that behind our behavior is a logic that guides and generates our actions. Unless we can change our inner logic, our outward changes will be limited and short-lived.

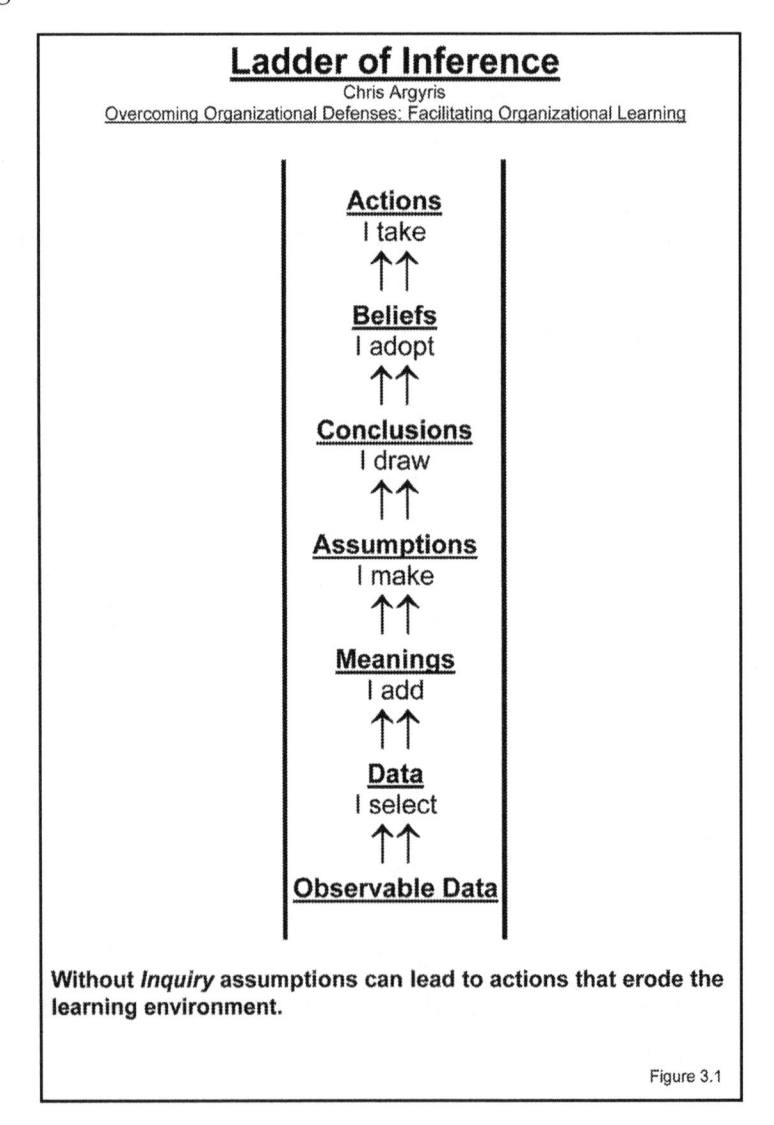

Ladder of Inference
Chris Argyris
Overcoming Organizational Defenses: Facilitating Organizational Learning

Actions
I take
↑↑
Beliefs
I adopt
↑↑
Conclusions
I draw
↑↑
Assumptions
I make
↑↑
Meanings
I add
↑↑
Data
I select
↑↑
Observable Data

Without *Inquiry* assumptions can lead to actions that erode the learning environment.

Figure 3.1

A model that has proved very helpful to us in understanding this concept is Chris Argyris' Ladder of Inference. In this model, we begin by recognizing that all around us every day is a plethora of *data*. While a facilitator works with groups, there is an enormous number of things a facilitator could pay attention to, i.e., people talking, shifting in their chairs, their body language, the hum of the air conditioning, the lights, noise from outside the room. Since we cannot focus on everything at once, we *select* certain things to pay attention to. Once we have selected something to focus our attention on, we quickly begin to give *meaning* to those things. The meaning we give is based on our experience, culture and training. With some meaning attached, we begin to make *assumptions* about the things we are focusing on. Again, our mental models about who we are and how the world works are automatically engaged. We may or may not be aware of the assumptions we are making. Yet the assumptions we make lead us to draw certain *conclusions* about the thing or person we are focusing on. This leads us to form certain *beliefs*, which generate our *actions* or *behavior*. All of this happens in a split second, yet the logic behind the behavior will continue to create the same kinds of behavior over time.

Here is an example. If we are working with a group and see someone leaning back in his chair with his arms folded, this posture can mean a couple of things. It could indicate someone who is skeptical and withdrawn from the group process. Or it could also indicate someone who is very comfortable and attentive. Based on our experience with this person or other people in groups who lean back and fold their arms, we will formulate some assumptions about this person. Depending on the assumptions that we form and the conclusions we draw, we will either treat this person as a skeptic to win over or an engaged participant who wants to learn something. What the Ladder of Inference allows us to do is to be fully aware of how we are choosing to see the person, that we are making those choices, whether we realize it or not.

The point of this discussion is that if we want to facilitate sustainable change or learning with a group or an individual, we need to help him or her surface his or her assumptions. If a person can become aware of his or her assumptions and challenge them, he or she will behave differently because it makes sense to act differently. Not only that, but since people tend to see those things that confirm what they already believe and dismiss those things that contradict what they believe, if we can help a person change his or her assumptions, he or she will change what they see and pay attention to in his or her environment. As facilitators, we will know that a group or individual is learning in a way that will lead to long-term effectiveness if they are becoming aware of their assumptions and in turn adopting more accurate assumptions.

As a sidebar, our assumptions are automated, taken-for-granted ways of understanding ourselves and our world. Consequently, they are not always accessible to us directly. What we think or say we believe is not always consistent with what we really believe. What we really believe comes from our assumptions. So, to become aware of our assumptions, we need some pathways that will bring our assumptions into our consciousness. We suggest at least two that we have at our constant disposal. The first is our actions, and the second is our emotions.

This first pathway seems the most obvious. What we do can be witnessed by others, and the consequences of our actions and decisions are usually observable. Consequently, by reflecting on our experiences and asking questions that seek to understand the 'why behind the what' of our actions, we are able to uncover the assumptions driving the actions. This explains the emphasis on reflection in some of the most innovative organizational and human learning writing of the last two decades.[1]

> **Actions and emotions provide the reflective facilitator the pathways to understand the assumptions or inner logic of individuals and groups.**

What may not be as obvious is the usefulness of our emotions as a pathway to understand our thinking. The relationship between emotions and thinking has been around for years.[2] Many of us have been taught not to trust emotion. It is irrational and uncontrollable. But no matter how irrational an emotion may be, it will always tell you what you believe to be true in that moment.

Actions and emotions provide the reflective facilitator the pathways to understand the assumptions or inner logic of individuals and groups. By asking questions such as, 'What does this action get for the performer of the action?' or 'Of all the possible emotional responses why does this response come now?,' the underlying logic can be surfaced.

Managing Differences

We often ask the question in seminars that we teach 'why people form teams?'. Most often, the response is because a group of people can be smarter and more effective than individuals. Yet teams most often never really maximize the perceived benefits that led them to be formed in the first place. Why? "Often when we listen to others we may discover that we are *listening from disturbance*; in other words, we are listening from an emotional memory rather than from the present moment."[3] Much of the lack of collective intelligence and collaboration is due to residual anxiety from previous personal conflicts. It may be a bad encounter with the person with whom one is trying to work. Or it can be a memory of another leader or team member from a previous team. The end result is that too often teams become dysfunctional because team members are too reactive to one another. Effective team members recognize and resist this temptation to listen from memory.

A second sign that individuals and teams are managing differences well is that the amount of tension and reactivity (automatic responses) diminishes and is replaced with purposeful listening and dialogue. When teams are practicing good Collective Learning, differences, rather than polarizing the team, are seen as opportunities to consider different perspectives. Consequently, the quality of decisions increases because the team is taking advantage of its collective intelligence.

In addition to diminished reactivity, learning teams are more aware of the choices they make. Rather than blame each other, circumstances, the facilitator or their leader for failure, learning teams seek to understand how each member contributed to ineffective action so that they can do better in the future.

Broadening Perspective

A third way to assess a team's learning status is how well team members let the perceptions of others broaden the team members' perspective. All of us, no matter how old we are, how intelligent we are or how educated we are, can see only a limited amount of the world around us. That is the limitation of being human. However, if a person considers the perspectives of those around the individual and does not get lost in defending or debating those perspectives, then that person can expand his or her understanding of himself or herself and the world. Learning teams do not waste their energy debating who has the right perceptions of an event. Rather, they take each person's perceptions as valuable and allow the different perspectives to provide a more complete picture of how things are. In this way, the breadth of experience on the team makes the team exponentially smarter.

Conclusion

Learning is the key to sustainable teams. Yet it is important to realize that learning goes beyond just assimilating new information or data. The learning necessary of new generation teams requires a deeper learning. The type of learning requires an ever-growing awareness of one's assumptions as well as the shared assumptions of the team. In addition, individuals and teams must become more intentional, especially when it comes to differences. The differences among the team members are the team's greatest potential strength and the source of its greatest struggles. When teams become aware of their assumptions and focus on being less reactive to ideas and practices that are different from what they are used to, teams will develop the ability to learn collectively, which will result in broader, more accurate perspectives of the world and work they must engage.

Chapter 4
The Dynamics of Collective Learning

"Americans learn only from catastrophes not from experience."
Theodore Roosevelt, *26th U.S. President*

In a world that moves as rapidly as ours, the concept of team must keep pace with the times. In this chapter, we will define a model that can provide a map for making sense out of the complex human interactions within teams. The model suggests that there are four phases that an individual or team moves through as it matures and learns. These phases are Disturbance, Chaos, Letting Go and Learning (see Figure 4.1). In addition, there are four core abilities that provide a reference for what is most important to participate in the dynamics of Collective Learning. These four core abilities are emotional awareness, critical reflection, courage and systems thinking.[1] Emotional awareness leads us to understand the power of emotions and their interaction in creating our behavior. Much of the illogical behavior that arises within teams can be explained in terms of emotional dynamics. Critical reflection pays attention not only to the obvious elements of an experience but also seeks understanding at the level of assumptions, values and beliefs. Courage is closely related to emotional awareness and is referred to in Chapter 5 as emotional stamina. It is the ability to be comfortable with discomfort. It is a quality that hangs in there during the difficult times that are encountered in our interactions with others. Systems thinking is the final ability. It sees the interconnectedness of things and is referred to in Chapter 6 as relational awareness. It is an understanding that relationships are the fundamental essence of the universe. For the facilitator or leader who wants to influence the effective interaction among a team, this model provides a frame of reference for making sense of team dynamics. The model also provides a place of reference for a facilitator to identify where an individual or team is and then develop ways to help the team move.

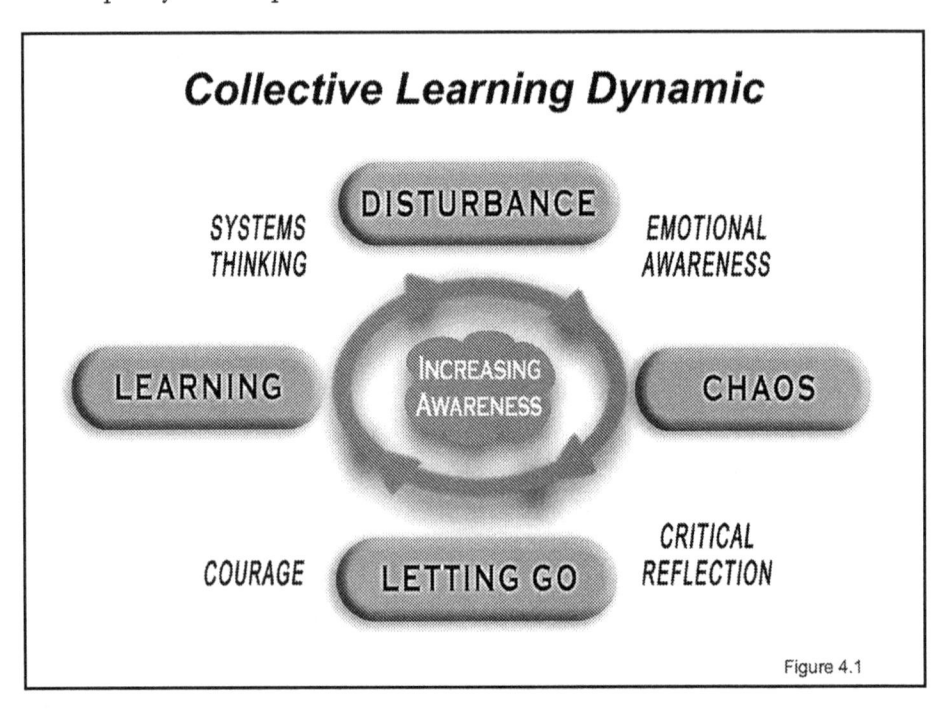

Collective Learning Dynamic

- SYSTEMS THINKING
- DISTURBANCE
- EMOTIONAL AWARENESS
- LEARNING
- INCREASING AWARENESS
- CHAOS
- COURAGE
- LETTING GO
- CRITICAL REFLECTION

Figure 4.1

In the previous chapter, the point was made that teams of this new generation must be adept at continuous learning and adaptation if they expect to thrive. Consistent with this point, the model for assessing team dynamics that will be explored in this chapter does not describe an end state that a group of people should try to achieve. Rather, the model is a map that describes the continuous dynamics of individuals and teams as they seek to be successful in the world. In addition, it is not the assertion of this model that every member of a team must be in the same place (phase) at the same time. This would ignore the polarity of individuality so necessary for successful teams. Contemporary teams must come to realize that teamwork, i.e., collaboration, is not a structure—it is a mindset. Collaboration is more than cooperation or sharing information.

Collaboration is having enough personal character and maturity to influence others who would pursue a common goal with you and to allow them to influence you. Thus, Collective Learning is about understanding how to interact with any collective of people, whether it is a team, a meeting, a congregation or even a family. Collective Learning is a choice to participate in a particular way with others. The job of the facilitator or leader is to help others come to make sense of their experience so that they can intentionally choose to be influenced by others and thus come to see things in a new way.

Disturbance

As facilitators, if our job is to help teams spend the majority of their time learning rather than something else, we must understand the dynamics of learning and how that learning can be derailed. Most, if not all, learning begins with a disturbance. What we mean by disturbance is *that something happens around or within us that signals that it is time to change.* An external disturbance could be new directives from one's boss, a new child, a changing economy or an interesting comment from a friend. The disturbance is external because these types of disturbances happen in the world around us and initiate from the actions or decisions of others. An internal disturbance can be a creative thought that we have, a sense of curiosity about how things work or just the nagging suspicion that there is a better way to do things. Internal disturbances start within us.

In a team, the most frequent source of disturbance is the differences among team members. Different perspectives and different ways of understanding an issue or solving a problem will disturb the team. Diversity is why we bring teams together, but then we are often surprised by that diversity.

Generally, this is one of the first places that people and teams begin to short-circuit the learning/change process. Disturbances occur but that does not always mean that they are considered. Disturbances are often troubling to people and teams. Consequently, the disturbances are often explained away, denied or just ignored. The hope is that if a disturbance is not acknowledged it will go away and no longer be a threat to the status quo. When this hope takes precedence, future improvement will be exchanged for momentary comfort.

Chaos

Once a disturbance is acknowledged, the next experience is generally some sort of uncertainty or chaos. Chaos can be intense or more like mild confusion. What you should recognize is that just because a team is experiencing some chaos does not mean that anything is wrong. Learning is about letting go of what is known to discover something not yet known. This process has some inherent uncertainty. People often experience this state as an emotion first. Consequently, people get anxious, tense and sometimes angry. Again, it is not the experience of chaos that signals a problem, it is how the team responds to the chaos.

The facilitator's role during chaos is to stay calm and not get caught up in the anxiety the team may be experiencing. Rather, the facilitator provides a sense of confidence in the team's ability to work through the chaos. The facilitator should also help the team members become aware of or clear about what they are really experiencing and the choices they are making in dealing with the chaos.

> **The facilitator should also help the team members become aware of or clear about what they are really experiencing and the choices they are making in dealing with the chaos.**

This is the second and most common place for teams to short-circuit their learning process. Below are some common ways individuals and teams relieve their tension and anxiety in the short run, which reduces their opportunity to learn and improve. These are all behaviors that a facilitator can look for as an indication of people who are stuck in the chaos phase.

Assume Control

When we are experiencing chaos, there is a natural tendency to try to regain a sense of security by trying to assume control. This effort can take a variety of forms within a group. A person can dominate the conversation as an attempt to assert some influence and regain a sense of control. A person can control critical resources so that he or she has a defined place of value with the team. A person can attempt to push his or her solution onto a group that is attempting to solve a problem. All of these actions have the same root cause and the same desired outcome. They come out of a sense of uncertainty, and their purpose is to help a person regain a sense of control.

Hero/Leader

In the midst of chaos, groups will often look for a leader to come and 'rescue' them. Rescuing them could be for someone to mandate a direction so that the chaos will subside. Greg once witnessed this very dynamic in a group of managers in a large corporation. They were engaged in an activity that created ambiguity and uncertainty. Among the group was the formal leader of the group. One woman was so unnerved by the uncertainty that she went over and stood by the leader's table, trying to get him to make a decision about the events happening back at her table. Her response to the chaos was to go and demand that the leader clarify the rules and make things clear. She was looking for a hero to solve her own uncertainty by forcing a set of behaviors on the situation. That is what we look for in the hero/leader—someone who will unilaterally remove the chaos by fiat.

When a hero/leader does not step forward, then those leaders who are most available become the focus of the group's frustration. As facilitators, we need to realize that, in this state, groups will often look to us to change something to make them feel more comfortable. If we do not, then they will blame us for causing the chaos. During this time, facilitators must be most aware of themselves. No one likes to be attacked, but a facilitator who cannot stand the messiness of the chaos will rescue the group to relieve his or her own anxiety. The result will be groups whose tolerance for discomfort is diminished, along with their potential to learn and adapt.

Blaming

Another strategy for relieving the discomfort of chaos is to blame. Group members may blame each other, they may blame the leader, as we just discussed, and they often blame the circumstances around them for their current state. What we try to listen for at this stage is to what extent do the members look for something outside of themselves for a solution or an excuse. When a team is in chaos, the group members often belittle the activity they are engaged in or the topic they are discussing. By limiting the value of the activity or discussion, they can more easily dismiss it as irrelevant.

Get Busy

Often, in the tension of a chaotic stage, team members simply start doing things to burn off the emotional energy. The difficulty with this is that the activity is often not well-thought-out and can actually have nothing to do with the actions that they need to take to be successful. Consequently, when the direction does become clear, the anxious team members' work will be revealed as not essential, and feelings and egos will be damaged. This sets in motion another disturbance and a chaotic state that will further undermine the team's performance. The facilitator can help in this situation by helping the group understand the decisions that were made and why. Clarity is the facilitator's greatest gift to a team in chaos.

Organize

Teams in chaos will sometimes turn to organization as a short-term solution. Now, we are not saying that organization is bad, but when people use procedures to hide from the real discussions that need to occur, then organization is a shortcut to dysfunction. Often the form this takes in groups is a vote. Voting becomes an expedient way out of a difficult decision. The problem with this is that the team loses vital dissenting perspectives that could help the team form the best decision.

Withdraw

Some groups and individuals cannot take the discomfort of chaos and choose to withdraw. Greg once was working with a group on a challenge course. The group was having some difficulty deciding a course of action, and as you might expect, a good deal of chaos was occurring. He noticed that one man had gotten off the platform the group was working on and had gone over to sit on the side. Greg asked the man what he was thinking. He said, "This is the way it always goes. They will beat each other up in there, and when they get tired, I will go back and participate again." For him, taking a seat on the sidelines was a preferable strategy for the tension of chaos. One of this man's "ah-ha moments" was that withdrawal also plays a significant role in the dysfunction of a team. Only by creatively engaging the chaos and using it as a catalyst for new solutions can a team or individual find sustainable solutions.

Quick Agreement

Frequently, individuals will quickly agree with one another to relieve their discomfort. A facilitator can tell this is happening because there will not be any dissenting perspectives taken seriously. In the anxiety of chaos, sameness provides a false sense of security. The outcome will be either a poor decision or a false agreement that will later unravel, damaging the trust among the team members.

The bottom line is that chaos is a natural part of learning. Facilitators must do a couple of things to help the team move forward. The facilitator should teach the group about chaos and the signs of taking the shortcut. This helps enroll the team as partners with the facilitator and minimizes the confrontational tone that could develop between the team and facilitator. The second thing a facilitator should do is stay very close and very visible to the team. The team members will need the reassurance that comes from a confident, available facilitator to help them weather the chaos. Ultimately, through asking questions and making observations, a facilitator can help the group gain some clarity about the real causes of their chaos. With this awareness, the team will be in a much better place to take the next steps to an effective action rather than a reactive one.

Letting Go

The steps from chaos to learning are not easy and require a good deal of courage. The path to learning requires a very counterintuitive action. Rather than follow the natural inclinations to hang on tighter in the midst of chaos, a facilitator who wants to create the atmosphere for learning must let go. Letting go is not about giving up one's ability to choose. Letting go also doesn't mean that the individual or the team members will just let whatever happens to them happen. Rather, letting go means to loosen one's grip to make space and opportunity for something new to emerge. Letting go is a conscious choice to not rely on things that normally provide security. Letting go is being open to new ideas and new possibilities and to be influenced by others. Letting go is the realization that there is a need for individuals and the group to "empty themselves of barriers to communication."[2]

> *Rather than follow the natural inclinations to hang on tighter in the midst of chaos, a facilitator who wants to create the atmosphere for learning must let go.*

What are those things that most individuals and teams need to let go of to create the openness for mutual influence so necessary for learning? The following list is not exhaustive, but it will provide facilitators some ideas for thinking about this question.

Ego

One of the first things that must go is the ego. If a team is to reach its maximum potential, members of that team must serve something greater than their individual self-interest. Learning requires the potential for mistakes and perhaps failures. An over-inflated ego will never be able to risk such possibilities. Consequently, only sure things will be considered.

Control

The struggle for control is at the heart of many team conflicts. In fact, a very common name for a stage of team development is Storming.[3] During this Storming stage, each team member is determining their own ability to influence the team, as well as how much control they are willing to give to others. The illusion that many follow is that they can and should control their environment. So, team members will try to control their circumstances, resources, information, the conversation and, most importantly, each other. This leads immediately to a great deal of resistance and tension. No one likes to be controlled. In the Letting Go phase of our model, the truth that counters this illusion of control is the realization that the greatest security does not come from trying to control others. The greatest security comes from the ability to control oneself and to learn. If I can figure out what I think and what my choices are, I can be confident in most situations.

Comfort

Learning is not always comfortable. It requires the ability to say I do not know or I need some help. Learning requires people to see things differently from the way they have always made sense of things. People who have a high need to always feel comfortable will not learn. When the emotional tension of new ideas and new ways of doing things surface, they will retreat back into what is safe rather than explore a new possibility. People with a high need for comfort will not risk the conflict of asking someone to explain his or her thinking on an issue or to suggest a new idea. Learning is a courageous act that demands that we relinquish our need for comfort.

Certainty

By certainty, we mean a couple of things. First, we are suggesting that we must let go of our need to be right. This need to be right turns most conversations into debates with each side is trying to win. Never mind that what is being fought over is not in the best interest of the team. What is most important is winning the point. Consequently, people will not listen to each other for they will be far too busy trying to formulate their next answer. Learning is primarily about sharing our ignorance. Our best questions come out of what we do not yet know.

Second, letting go of certainty means letting go of the need to always know how things will work out. We often see teams and individuals who will not make a move because they do not know exactly how things will work out. There are many necessary and profound conversations that never occur because the parties involved do not know where the dialogue might take them. People who really learn are willing to take risks. In fact, how can we ever really take hold of something new unless we are willing to let go of what we are currently holding onto?

Past Experience

Too many times we do not listen to people because of some past experience. We frequently listen from memory rather than in the current moment. What we mean is that we have many past experiences that are associated with very strong feelings. When people in our presence elicit one of these feelings, we often shut off our conscious minds and simply start responding automatically. In other words, we are listening to the current conversation from memory.

Pre-conceived Solutions

It is very common for individuals on a team to approach a project or problem to solve with some idea of how it should be done. There is nothing wrong with this as long as there is openness to new perspectives or holes in our solutions. This is particularly limiting when it is combined with a need to be right. All conversations will lead to confrontation or very subtle attempts to convert others to the one solution. Anything that does not confirm that solution is automatically dismissed.

There will be many particular things that specific groups may need to let go of if they are to learn to interact differently. We have found it useful at times to have the team spend some time expressing what they need to let go of. We do this because it provides some clarity to where the team is trying go and makes it easier for people to not get stuck in old habits.

Implications of the Model

So what are the implications of this model for teams and facilitators? There are several ideas that have emerged that have fundamentally changed the way we work with teams.

The first implication is that this model has changed the way we understand *shared leadership* in a team setting. In the traditional way of thinking, leadership was about being in charge. Now that did not necessarily mean that the person in charge was a tyrant, but someone had to be giving directions. In some models, the playing out of this taking charge was the driver behind the storming or chaotic stage of team development. So if leadership was being in charge, how could teams effectively share that leadership? If team members rotate leadership based on the day or some kind of random selection process, how could the team ensure that the right person was in charge at the right time? On the other hand, if leadership is thought of as influence, then shared leadership could look entirely different.[4] There may be someone who comes to the forefront of influence, but the role (not a position) is given to that person because the individual has the clearest vision of where the team is heading. In addition, each person can have significant influence on the team by understanding the dynamics of Collective Learning. A portion of the leadership role is making sure that the team and each member are continuing to move through the learning cycle. For instance, if the team members, due to their discomfort, have quickly agreed on a decision, but they are overlooking some vital information, a person could act as a disturbance. By making something known that is not being considered, that person has had a role in leading the team. So leadership becomes a matter of who has the awareness and courage to try to influence the team toward a more complete and healthy process of learning. Additional roles of leaders can include clarifying the final results so that everyone knows the direction, being a non-anxious presence in the midst of a chaotic period and being willing to demonstrate some vulnerability to strengthen the level of trust in the group. In this way of thinking, leadership is a role that one or many can play rather than a position to which everyone should submit.

A second implication of this dynamic way of viewing teams is that it changes the way we think about **diversity** in teams. Some of the traditional methods of building teams tried to put things in place to minimize the differences on a team. Differences cause conflict or at least they can if a team is not prepared to value difference. If learning, that is, the continuous act of making sense of what is happening and continuing to adapt to be more effective, is the core work of teams, then it is a necessity that there is enough disturbance in their environments. Differences, whether coming as difference of perspective among team members or feedback from a third party, are the critical source of disturbance for teams and individuals. As facilitators, we want to make sure that the team is prepared to value and pay attention to these disturbances when they occur and we must look at the environment of the team to make sure the team members will have the necessary input for growth. So it will not be good enough that the team members have respect for each other and can work together well. They also need to have a clear picture of their end result and a way of monitoring their progress. A critical role for a facilitator to play is being a disturbance for this team. This may not always be the most comfortable role, but it is critical for the team's development.

> *So leadership becomes a matter of who has the awareness and courage to try to influence the team toward a more complete and healthy process of learning.*

A third implication of understanding Collective Learning is the recognition that the **emotional process** and **presence** of the leaders are more important than technique. If we can focus on only a single thing with team leaders, it is not teaching them techniques to manage the symptoms of a poorly functioning team. Rather, it is equipping that leader to be aware of his or her own anxieties and their hidden assumptions and learn how to rise out of the anxieties of the team while staying connected to the team. Presence or the way a leader responds to stress and anxiety will do more in the long run to ensure team health than any technique. Presence is contagious. As a leader demonstrates a value for disturbance and is vulnerable (open for real learning), the team will come to appreciate these things as well. Leaders, including facilitators, often must provide the courage and will for the team to stick with the learning process at the beginning. When they do, they will need far fewer techniques to help the team function well.

Conclusion

If the team manages the disturbances, does not panic in chaos and is courageous enough to let go of those things that make them ineffective, then the team can channel its energy into learning. We need to recognize that learning is not the end game. This is why the model is a circle rather than a straight line. With learning comes new disturbances. The good news is that as individuals and teams become more adept at learning, they get faster at it. Disturbances are not ignored, but rather are anticipated, even sought after. Energy is not wasted on holding onto control. A new level of confidence can take hold because the team members are now equipped to go anywhere they need to go. Shared leadership becomes a natural response to team challenges. In the end, the team is poised to be self-assessing, self-correcting and self-renewing.

Chapter 5
Critical Opportunities for Facilitators

"So, what's behind our failure of will to change in profound ways?"
L.A. Fitzgerald - "Living on the Edge"

Facilitators help teams because they are able to stand back and observe the interaction of the team through the lens of the four phases of the model explained in the last chapter. Observations alone, however, are not enough. Another critical role for facilitators is to intervene. The goal of the intervention is that the team or at least some members discover something they have not been able to see. Intervention is not about getting a group to do what you want them to do. Lasting change comes when a new way of acting grows out of a new perspective of one's self and others. This chapter outlines critical opportunities for intervention to assist teams in developing their Collective Learning skills.

Change involves new behavior and different ways of thinking, but what will limit this effort is the emotional processes involved. Of all the emotions, the one most damaging is fear. Fear is an ever-present antagonist seeking to draw us into well-rehearsed but very limited responses to threat and stress. Any number of situations can arouse anxiety: uncertainty, ambiguity, complexity, embarrassment and the awkwardness that comes from something new. If we do not learn to acknowledge and manage our responses driven by fear, we will never truly change, and our abilities to be creative and innovative will remain hidden.

A concrete example might help confirm this idea. Remember the earlier example in the Introduction to this book about a group on a challenge course? The group had made great progress in the debrief after a particular element. The group members had identified things that were limiting their teamwork and had solid suggestions for improvement. We walked from one event to the next, and while solving the problems at the new event, the group members acted as if they had never talked together, let alone worked together. Why the setback? The only thing different with the second element was a time limit. This one difference created enough anxiety in the group that the group members forgot all they had just talked about.

So what behavior should the facilitator be watching for to help develop the team's Collective Learning skills? What should the team be made aware of? The place to begin is to ask yourself, *What typically causes teams to struggle?* Power struggles, conflict, apathy, disconnection, dominating individuals, poor planning and over-talking are all common difficulties. The next question you must ask yourself is, *Do I want to help teams manage their symptoms or help them get to the root issues so that they can solve their problems and not just mask the symptoms?* If the answer is to really solve their problems, then the place for a facilitator to focus is anxiety and those things that sustain it. Most groups possess the creativity to find their own solutions, but when the team members are stressed and their anxiety is raised, the team loses its capability to think clearly. The team members become focused on finding security. Anxiety is like pouring water on a perfectly good microchip. Even though the circuitry is perfect, the water shorts the chip out. This is the limiting effect of anxiety. So the first step in formulating an intervention is to understand the nature of anxiety—what amplifies it and what dissipates it.

> **So the first step in formulating an intervention is to understand the nature of anxiety—what amplifies it and what dissipates it.**

According to Amussen,[1] anxiety can be experienced as a chronic condition or an acute event. Typically, chronic anxiety is the result of repeated patterns of behavior or existing conditions in the team's environment. For instance, a team that is consistently without direction, whose leader is distant and removed, will have a continuously raised level of anxiety. The critical thing to understand is that this one condition may not be enough to disable a team. What chronic anxiety does is diminish some of the team's ability to deal with other things. When the team members experience multiple chronic conditions, the team may become dysfunctional. Typically, an absent leader also leads to a host of other conditions that amplify or sustain chronic anxiety. Resolving this type of anxiety is generally a process that requires a number of interventions not only with the team members but with the larger organization.

On the other hand, acute anxiety results from a distinct stressful event. It can be something bad, such as being fired or conflict with a co-worker. It can also be a challenge, such as a new project. Sometimes, teams that are stuck are only experiencing a momentary pit because a specific event has exhausted their ability to handle anxiety. In these cases, a facilitator can be very helpful by suggesting the team step away from the challenge to gain better perspective and/or provide some process for the team to work through the next steps.

The important thing is for the facilitator to watch for patterns of actions that amplify anxiety. This will indicate a more chronic type of team anxiety and will in all likelihood require a longer term for working with the team.

With all this in mind, the critical question still remains—what does a facilitator look for? Think back to our section on chaos in Chapter 4 and the less effective methods for dealing with it. We suggest that all seven of those described behaviors amplify the anxiety in the team. For a while, they may allow some measure of relief for some members of the team, but the overall team anxiety is likely to increase. This is because fleeing out of chaos leaves something unsaid, undone or unnoticed.

Other signals of potential anxiety include unilateral decisions that affect the whole, secrecy, lack of direction, leaders who over-function or assume responsibility for things that rightfully belong to another and teams that are constantly trying to change each other.[2] When there is an atmosphere of "willing others to change," there will be a heightened sense of anxiety as well as a lowered sense of personal responsibility.

We want to explore this last idea in more detail. In M. Scott Peck's book *The Different Drum*, he describes the attempt to "will others to change." In response to the anxiety caused by the emerging awareness of the differences among the group members, Peck tells us there will often be a high degree of "healing and converting":

> In the stage of chaos, individual differences are ... right out in the open. Only now, instead of trying to hide or ignore them, the group is attempting to obliterate them. Underlying the attempts to heal and convert is not so much the motive of love as the motive to make everyone normal—and the motive to win, as members fight over whose norm might prevail. [3]

As long as team members believe their success is tied to changing another member, they will continue to amplify the anxiety. They will push, threaten, manipulate and seduce those whom the rest believe need to change. Either way the team member responds, his or her anxiety will go up. Either the team members will succumb to the pressure to conform, or they will be viewed as selfish and egotistical. The former action will send the message that it is not okay to have your own thoughts and ideas. As the facilitator, this tendency typically presents itself with the group or the individual members generally looking outside their own power for a solution to their current condition.

In the end, these actions are really just manifestations of what we believe to be the root causes of team anxiety. At the root of this emotional chaos are self-doubt, a lack of trust and a fear of differences. Self-doubt grows out of a lack of confidence and courage. People who are insecure tend to be less clear about what they believe and, more importantly, why they believe it. They tend to be more susceptible to trying to take control or to be manipulated by others. People with a poor sense of self also have difficulty with trusting others. Trust requires a willingness to be vulnerable and often accompanies leaps of faith. To the insecure person, the discomfort with not being certain and/or being in control is too much. Trust may be earned after a while, but it will always remain fragile for trust depends on the actions of others rather than the choice of the individual. Finally, when insecurity and a lack of trust exist, there is usually a fear of differences.

When people feel anxious, they are motivated toward togetherness. In other words, the more a group is alike, the more secure everyone feels because things are more predictable and familiar. This works only to a point. If the team moves too much toward the togetherness end of the continuum, individuals begin to feel overwhelmed and will be driven toward individuality. Practically speaking, difference will be feared and seen as a problem. Anyone who attempts to have a different idea or to think for himself or herself will be seen as threatening, selfish and not a team player. So individuals will be pressed to agree, which causes some to experience a lack of authenticity. Consequently, their anxiety is raised along with the group's.

Differentiation

One of the most helpful concepts we have come across in understanding anxiety and the emotional processes of individuals and groups comes from the field of family therapy. Family Systems Theory, which originated in the work of Dr. Murray Bowen, recognized that anxiety is the single greatest threat to healthy relationships. When a relationship is stressful, the resulting anxiety tends to make individuals reactive. Bowen believed if people could slow down their inner processes and become aware of the scripts they enact, new choices could be made. He called this process differentiation.

There are two foundational ideas that help provide a backdrop for understanding self-differentiation. First, there are two forces that continually pull at every person, which are the same forces of the fear of differences we previously discussed. One is to be an individual, to think for oneself, to determine whom one is and to make one's own choices. Opposite this is the desire to be together, to belong and to be a part of a group. The second force stands opposed to the first in that the tendency to be together entices us to not think for ourselves, but to let the group define who we are. The result is that individuals live their lives reacting to other people.

This leads to the second foundational idea. When people feel stressed or anxious, they will revert to a base-level response. These responses are automatic and reactive. Reactivity is a knee-jerk response to situations we perceive as threatening. The threat could be possible failure or embarrassment. The threat is anything that seems to de-stabilize our current sense of control and security.

When such conditions exist, our anxiety is very high. From the time we are very young, we learn strategies for dealing with threats. As we get older, our defensive scripts become second nature. We never think about them, and they go into action automatically. Reactivity is the water that shorts out the relational systems we are in. Most of the chronic social problems in groups are caused by this reactivity. Blame, avoidance, hidden agendas and posturing are all knee-jerk responses to anxious situations.

Although there are an infinite number of manifestations these scripts can take, at their root they are all a variation of the fight or flight reaction. This leads to people either running away from their anxiety or being stuck in unproductive responses used over and over and that have some hint of violence.

To clarify, we are not necessarily referring to a physical violence, but rather an attempt to defend oneself or to subdue the threat by a force of will. Voyer, Gould and Ford refer to the work of Bion in which he describes this fight or flight instinct, as either blaming others or pretending there is no issue.[4] The result of this kind of process is the root of the impotence of most change efforts.

> **Self-differentiated members can regulate their anxiety and not resort to manipulative or hurtful actions to find comfort.**

The solution for the anxious team is to promote those attitudes and actions that dissipate the anxiety rather than amplify it. In the end, promoting learning at the individual and group levels will result in lower anxiety. Self-differentiated leadership is one of the ways to calm the chronic anxiety of a team.

Self-differentiated people are individuals who know what they think, can take a stand when challenged, who do not overreact to others and can see things in a new or different light. Self-differentiated members can regulate their anxiety and not resort to manipulative or hurtful actions to find comfort. Consequently, they become leaders because they can influence the outcome for the team. These leaders do not require formal positions or require others to be like them. This freedom allows team members to make up their own minds. **Promoting personal**

responsibility rather than blaming is the first key intervention for facilitators dealing with anxiety.

A second critical mechanism for facilitators to help reduce anxiety is to encourage **clear direction**. It is always surprising to me how many teams take action without really knowing where they are going. Some teams function for long periods of time just solving the next problem or finishing the next task. Without a clear sense of direction, teams will not know how well they are doing, if they are being effective, what adaptations to their current plan need to be made or how to take personal initiative.

Here is an example of the impact of this condition. Greg was working with a team that had completed a good deal of discussion concerning this rather complicated exercise the team was to accomplish. The initial part of the work required that a few of the team members be out of earshot from the rest of the team. The first few tasks of the project took longer than expected. As time wore on, the remaining members grew more and more anxious about being behind schedule. They had no idea why things were taking so long. In the absence of information (and the absence of a clear picture of their final results), some team members began working on new tasks not originally included in the plan. They were working hard, and their activity eased their anxiety of waiting. Finally, the first tasks were completed, and the rest of the plan began to be implemented, only now there were two directions in motion. The team members who had decided to act on their own had completed some work. In the end, this new and additional work was recognized as unnecessary. This offended the portion of the team who had worked on this work. They took the decision to not use their work personally. They had invested their time, talent and energy, and it was just being tossed aside. Consequently, their anxiety went through the roof. It continued to cause the team difficulty because those team members could not let go of the rejection of their effort.

The teams that tend to be the most effective and adaptable are teams that clearly define their end result. With this shared direction, all the team members can take action in parallel process because they all are committed to their end destination. Individuals can take personal initiative while not damaging the collective direction because individual decisions can be measured against the end result. When this is combined with high levels of competence, mutual trust in that competence and frequent communication, teams are very resilient and successful.

Facilitators and Non-anxious Presence

The goal of differentiation for facilitators is to make people aware of their internal processes as they are happening. Early on, this may be difficult for some. The facilitator then becomes a very real asset. If the facilitator does not react to what is happening in the group, and can stay connected to the group, then he or she can be a non-anxious presence. Think of it as providing a faith in the process until the group can believe in it as well. There are two parts to this role. First, the facilitator must be aware of his or her own inner processes so as not to react to the group. Often, when groups are going through the Storming stage of group development, they blame the facilitator. A reactive response would be for the facilitator to accept the blame and try to relieve the stress in the group. He or she may do this by becoming authoritarian or by letting the group out of the circumstance that is revealing the stress. A non-reactive response would be to acknowledge that the group is struggling, but to help the group take responsibility for the process. This is accomplished by helping the group members discover what is at the root of their anxiety. It should be said often these attempts to make the facilitator responsible for the group's anxiety come as either sabotage (attacks that are either overt or covert) or seduction (trying to get the facilitator to act out of feelings of friendship or loyalty).

The second aspect of the non-anxious presence is to stay connected and involved in the relationships. When the anxiety in the group is high, it is very easy for the facilitator to distance himself from the group. At the extreme end of this continuum is emotional cutoff or breaking off the relationship altogether. However, if the facilitator sees himself as above or different from the group, then distancing has occurred. This attitude can also take the form of blame or scolding.

Greg once participated in an expedition where this scolding attitude occurred. The group had just about reached its limit in every way, and the group members blamed the leader. The leader, who was offered an excellent opportunity to join them in their suffering, instead chose to scold the group members and blame the entire situation on their poor attitudes. Furthermore, she compared them with other groups she had led, and revealed how unsatisfactory this group was. She cut herself off from the group's anxiety. Although the end result was not entirely the facilitator's fault, the group remained a fragmented collection of individuals for the remainder of the trip. If she had been a non-anxious presence, the group members could have really formed some cohesion.

Team members who have been subject to a high degree of chronic anxiety will generally talk at each other, but rarely do they truly listen. The need to somehow accomplish something (remember busyness can be a short-term emotional release for anxiety) constantly makes the team feel pressured. Another intervention to begin to dissipate this emotional pressure is through **collective reflection.** Collective reflection is a structured process by which team members reflect on their experience to make meaning of that experience, learn from that experience and identify the next steps necessary to succeed. There are many models for doing this type of reflection. The particular technique is not as important as developing the mindset that says the best actions come out of reflection. Slowing down allows for emotions to wane and critical thinking to begin. Of all the team members, the leader of the team needs to understand this. He or she will set the tone that allows for dialogue and shared reflection to take place. Remember, in this process shared reflection is as much an emotional shift as an intellectual or behavioral one. Team members must stop, wait and calm themselves to allow their best ideas to take shape.

Much of the time, a team's anxiety comes from simply not knowing what is happening or how decisions are made. In this void of not knowing, many rumors blossom. The response to this is to develop **transparency** of the team. Transparency simply means that decisions are made in the open, with some kind of known process and criteria. Decisions are not made in secret and followed up by unilateral actions. Decisions have some logic to them, and those who made the decisions take ownership for the decisions. This is not to say that everyone is involved in every decision. Rather, team members know how decisions get made and whether all parties affected by the decision should be included at some level.

Finally, **inclusiveness** also dissipates anxiety. By inclusiveness, we mean the appreciation and valuing of differences. Since difference is often a triggering event in the emotional process of individuals and teams, learning to appreciate that difference is a significant milestone. Again, the first step in this process is awareness of the tendency of people to dismiss that which is different from themselves. This is an emotional response to reestablish the perception of security. In addition, teams learn that difference does not mean that which has been is wrong. If members hear different points of view as condemning their own perception, confrontation will soon follow. Inclusiveness recognizes two important ideas. The first is there is enough for all.[5] Everyone can succeed. Everyone can contribute. Everyone has something valuable to offer. Second, differences are valuable disturbances that can lead to innovation and learning.

> *The first step in this process is awareness of the tendency of people to dismiss that which is different from themselves.*

Here is an example of inclusiveness. Greg was working with a group in a challenge course program. One of the elements the team had to cross was a series of cables a few feet off the ground that formed a "V" called the Wild Woosey. As one moves away from the entry point, the cables diverge, growing wider at the opposite end. This group had established a process that was working for most of the members. However, a couple of people simply could not use the established process. Most teams in this situation try to coach or insist that everyone figure out the process. The person or persons unable to use the process become the focus of the team's effort as the team tries to encourage (a.k.a. force) the team member to conform. This team was different. The team members simply used their physical limitations to innovate and improve their process. They did not make this a big deal. Those involved in the element at the time took the best of what had been working and adjusted it to the needs of those on the element. In the end, they discovered a way that was very easy for all and much more efficient than the process they had started with. The appreciation of differences led this team to learn and succeed rather than amplify the collective anxiety.

Triangles

This chapter has suggested ways facilitators can help groups deal with anxiety. There will be anxiety in groups, and as facilitators, we will have to deal with it. The question is, *Will we deal with it intentionally?* In this final section, we want to identify a very common and unintentional strategy used to deal with anxiety. Unintentional because very few people consciously create this structure. It is one of those reactive scripts that offer us a quick relief of tension, but in reality only perpetuates the problem.

The strategy we are talking about is called Triangling, and it works like this: Two people find themselves in a conflictual relationship. The conflict may be acute or chronic, but it causes a sense of tension between the parties. Instead of the two people talking to each other, one or both bring another party into the situation. This could be talking about a situation with someone else to vent, or it could be finding a common enemy or crisis, which allows the two people in conflict to form a false partnership to address the crisis situation. This happens all the time. A couple gets in a fight, the wife calls mom and the husband complains to his buddies. Two different triangles have been formed. Sometimes a system may scapegoat a particular person and make the scapegoat the focus of hostility. The bottom line of a triangle is the responsibility for the tension is shifted from the two people in conflict to a third party. The real source of the anxiety is not dealt with, but is shifted somewhere else to make it more comfortable for the two in conflict.

We observe this in groups quite often. Think about a group that is polarized around a particular issue. Often, one or more sides try to get the facilitator to take a side. One of the faces of a triangle is the belief that if one person can get enough people on his or her side, they will win. If the facilitator tries to reason this kind of situation out, there will be little success. The reason is the problem is not primarily a problem of content but of process. The emotional process of a group exhibiting these behaviors is stuck, and no amount of information or technique will fix it. This can also help to explain why facilitators often get blamed for a group's struggle. If the group can scapegoat the facilitator, then the group members do not have to take responsibility for the struggle themselves. The group members can vent their frustration with each other by focusing on the facilitator. This creates a false alliance, and the tension being experienced is lowered within the group. The truth is that the real problem has not been dealt with, and the symptoms will show up again later.

Conclusion

Facilitators have limited time to make a difference with a team. We try to focus on those things that offer the greatest potential payoff.

Teaching teams to be aware of and how to manage their own anxiety equips them to solve many dilemmas. Just as balance equips us to ride a bike, a motorcycle or a skateboard, being able to recognize the assumptions team members are making and managing their individual and collective anxiety allows a team to tap into its best and most creative ideas and responses to challenges. We believe Family Systems Theory can really be helpful with this part of the equation. Fear or anxiety is a very real source of chronic relational problems. The discipline of differentiation can help to identify assumptions causing some tension. Differentiation also requires us to stay in the relationship so problems can be dealt with. Emotional stamina is crucial to the differentiation process. Without emotional stamina, a person will always opt for the easiest way out. Finally, we need to be conscious of developing triangles to relieve tension in a relationship. Triangling shifts the burden of relational anxiety only for the moment. As soon as the triangle is dissolved, the real tension will resurface. These are behaviors that a facilitator can look for in groups and help explain some of the mystery behind why intelligent groups become stuck.

Chapter 6
Relational Awareness

"All leadership begins with self-leadership, and self-leadership begins with knowing oneself."

Chris Lowney - <u>Heroic Leadership</u>

When individuals and teams intentionally apply the four core abilities during the four phases from Chapter 4 to grow and improve, we call it Process Facilitation. When Greg began working on integrating these ideas from all the fields and research in the early 1990s, he realized there was no single term to describe what it would look like to apply these abilities. Consequently, he called the concept Process Facilitation. Process connotes something that is ongoing, requiring constant attention. It is not a one-time event but a way of being. Not only is continuous attention necessary to learn and grow, but it is important to help those who are most adaptable do it intentionally. Facilitation is the word to describe this element of the dynamic. Process Facilitation requires intentional personal responsibility for the actions one chooses. (This is different from Edgar Schein's process consultation and process facilitation commonly discussed in organizational development circles.)[1]

The first step in developing Process Facilitation involves the way we see the world. Our old mechanistic paradigms see a world of isolated parts and direct cause and effect. The studies done involving systems have opened our eyes to other possible views of the world. An oversimplified summary of systems theory sees the world in terms of relationships and multiple causes. In this chapter, we will do two things. First, we will describe some ideas that have grown out of systems theory that are very helpful to facilitators. This will not be an exhaustive review of systems theory but rather some functional ideas that apply systems principles to groups. We will then present specific applications of this way of seeing the world.

Here's an exercise that will help contrast the linear, mechanistic view of the world and systems thinking.[2] The first part is to count the number of times the word flag appears in "The Star Spangled Banner." The second part of this exercise is to count the number of lamps in your living room. What was the difference in how you came to the answers of these questions? If you are like us, you sang each word of the song. This is a linear process. However, for the lamps, you pictured the room and envisioned where everything was in relation to everything else. It is the second process, seeing the parts in relation to the whole, that is the foundation of systems thinking.

Here is another concrete metaphor that might help with the abstract notion of systems thinking. When you go to the mall, how do you maintain a sense of direction? The method we use is to know where the big department stores are (since they are usually on the ends) and relate everything else to those stores. That is an example of thinking systemically. Again, systems thinking is about the way we perceive the world. This way of thinking helps us determine what we will pay attention to. It tells us that if we want to understand our world, we must think in terms of relationships.

Before we go much further, it would seem useful to define a system. A common definition is "whenever a group of elements is so interconnected that a change in one part produces a change in the whole structure, you have a system."[3] The key to a system is a collection of parts that are in relationship to one another. This means that your body is a system. You have many individual organs that relate to one another and influence one another. Your family is a system and so are your co-workers, your company, your church, your city, etc. This also means that every group that comes to a challenge course is a system. If we want to really understand what is going on in the group and why, there are four important ideas from systems thinking facilitators can explore.

Idea # 1 - The key to understanding the group is in the interactions between members.

Pretend you have never eaten a piece of apple pie in your life and you have asked us to help you understand apple pie. We put in front of you some flour, butter, water, baking soda, apples, sugar and cinnamon. How well would you understand apple pie? However, if we combined all of these ingredients and baked them for thirty minutes at 375 degrees and put that on the table in front of you, would you have a better understanding of apple pie?

Anytime we try to understand a system by looking only at individual parts, we will only see part of the truth. As we observe groups, we need to recognize the mutual influence all the individuals have on each other. Problems are never isolated in just one person. The source of solutions to human problems is in the relationships. Mechanistic thinking looks for simple, one-way cause-and-effect chains. This often results in blaming certain individuals. Blame limits the ability of team members to realize their own contributions to the group's process. Ultimately, seeking to place blame somewhere only undermines the team's ability to learn and grow. Individuals will always act like victims or at least resign themselves to the idea of 'nothing will ever change' since someone else must change in order for things to improve. Facilitators who buy into this idea will only perpetuate an ineffective team process.

> **Anytime we try to understand a system by looking only at individual parts, we will only see part of the truth.**

Systems thinking helps us realize that the source of the problem is not in one person but in the interactions of team members. Only when the facilitator can help groups see that every individual is contributing to the group process can any real intervention be accomplished. This is really an empowering idea. If the opportunity for change lies in the interactions between people, there is always someone I can change as a part of the interaction—me. Change is not dependent on getting someone else to change. As a matter of fact, if as a team member, I focus my energy on changing someone else, I will only undermine the trust of the team and create an undercurrent of resistance.

This way of perceiving the world helps the team in one other way. It goes a long way in removing much of the shame and guilt contained in admitting something is wrong. No longer do relationship struggles require someone to be right and someone to be wrong. The truth is all parties have some responsibility in the struggle whether it is direct or indirect. A direct contribution would be when something I am doing initiates a dysfunctional pattern. An indirect contribution would be if I tolerate or cover for someone else's behavior, thus perpetuating that person's lack of responsibility. If team members can view relationship struggles as something in which everyone makes a contribution, then they can search for solutions together. This also helps to build cohesion because it focuses attention on what the team members have in common.

Here's an example of how this type of thinking would look in a team session. Greg was recently working with a group whose leader, after being surprised by the team's feedback to a question, began to suppress the concerns being voiced. As Greg talked with some of the members of the group at lunch, it became apparent they had assigned the difficulties the team was experiencing solely to the leader. What the members failed to realize was that they had never told the leader what effect his actions were having on the team. If Greg had supported the group members in making the leader the scapegoat, Greg would have colluded with them to perpetuate the dysfunctional team dynamic. If Greg focused his attention on changing the leader, Greg might have influenced the symptom, but the underlying mistrust and anxiety of the group would have continued. Eventually, the underlying issue would be revealed in a different symptom. Instead, Greg asked the group to look at the interactions between the team and the leader. By asking questions about why the relationship existed as it did, a very open and honest dialogue began. The team experienced a tremendous breakthrough.

Facilitators will never be able to understand all the relationships of variables in a system. Systems are much too complex. However, the more we view groups as systems, the greater the likelihood our interventions will provide real opportunities for learning.

Idea #2 - In a system, the whole is greater than the sum of its parts.

This second idea is closely related to the first. Because systems are networks of relationships, one can never understand the system by looking only at the individual members. To do so is to remove the context that helps describe the members. To take this idea one step further, systems thinking would say the system itself tends to take on a persona as well. Through the work of people such as Argyris and Friedman, there is now the understanding that the collective group has many of the same attributes as the individuals who make up the group.[4] Groups have identities, made up of shared values and beliefs. These do not have to be articulated to influence the group's behavior. In fact, the shared identity is often not spoken of but rather operates as unspoken rules. Groups also have defensive scripts (automatic responses) for dealing with anxiety and are just as reactive as individuals. These scripts, when unnoticed, are very limiting for the group. The problem is the collective scripts cannot be understood by simply looking at the individuals. The collective scripts can only be understood within the context of the interactions of the members.

An illustration from field theory may help provide a clearer picture of this idea. Gravity is a force that occurs as bodies (planets, moons, etc.) come into relationships with one another. The bodies in relationship create the gravity; however, after the gravity field is created, the force of gravity has more influence on the individual elements than the elements have on the field. The same is true with human systems. Individuals come together to create a system. However, after the system is created, the collective beliefs, values and assumptions often have greater influence on the individuals than the individuals can have over the system. The result of all of this is that interventions cannot occur at the individual level only. There must be an increased awareness of the collective identity and behavior if sustained change is to occur. Otherwise, the system will always be undermining the change the individuals are trying to enact.

Idea #3 – Long-term solutions focus on root issues, not just the symptoms.

Within group settings, most of our attention is naturally focused on what is easiest to see. This is typical behavior. Interventions that intend to correct a behavior focus only on the symptom and not the root issue. Symptoms are the observable effects of inner processes. The inner processes are things such as feelings, beliefs and mental models. If true change is to occur, the facilitator must address the core issue. If the core issue is not addressed, the symptom may be removed, but the problem will resurface in another symptom sometime later. Senge reminds us that the "most insidious consequence of applying non-systemic solutions is increased need for more and more of the solution."[5] A very concrete example of this is when the facilitator must continue to remind the group to spot each other when on an element. The more the facilitator reminds, the more he or she has to keep reminding for the group to be safe. This strategy never addresses the real issue so the symptom never goes away. It also shifts the burden to the facilitator. The group is not dealing with its own symptom.

Here is a real-life story that models this idea. Greg was working with a group of high school students in a physical education class. One young man was totally disengaged from the group initiative. Greg walked over to him and began asking him his opinion of the group's effort. He thought they were not doing very well. When Greg asked why, the young man's response was it was a stupid game. Greg wanted to clarify if the young man thought the game was stupid or the group was stupid. The young man assured Greg it was the game. Greg thanked the young man for his insights and went back to observing the group. Within five minutes, the young man was completely engaged as a "quality control" person for the group. He made sure they were staying within the given boundaries. What was the reason for the change? We think it was because Greg allowed the young man to speak his mind and communicated to him that his ideas were valid and important. Greg could have simply demanded that the young man participate. Even if Greg had succeeded in making the young man conform, he would not have had any ownership of his contribution. In fact, his resentment of the entire program would most likely have increased, and Greg would had to have made the young man participate every time. Instead, he willingly changed his behavior and became an integral part of the group. Systemic solutions look at the why behind a problem and not simply the what.

> **Interventions that intend to correct a behavior focus only on the symptom and not the root issue.**

Idea #4 - Small changes over time can make a big difference.

One of the greatest faults of a facilitator is always looking for a home run—constantly trying to create the big breakthrough. Only in the last few years have we become aware that most great things have small beginnings. The old way of thinking viewed the world as a machine. Output equaled input. Science is telling us now that very small changes in a system can create very big differences. Scientists call it the Butterfly

Effect.[6] This is the theory that a butterfly flapping its wings in Japan can cause a tornado in California. Now whether that is really true we may never know. However, we do know from experience it is often a very small change that fundamentally affects a group's dynamics. It can be a different tone of voice, asking questions in a subtly different way or just making a slight change in perspective. For example, just suggesting that conflicts are caused by the mutual influences of two people on one another can transform a chronic strife into a challenge to overcome together. Facilitators should set their sights on making small differences in the team's process. Over time, it is unknown how big an influence that small difference might yield.

A friend of ours, and a fellow facilitator, tells a story that illustrates this point well. Edwin Moses was a world-class track star. Early in his career, he showed some real promise, but he had not had the breakthrough that would vault him to the top of his sport. He was winning many races and losing some as well. After one particular meet, a fan handed Edwin a videotape and asked him to watch it. He stuck it in his pocket with really no intention of watching it. That night at his hotel room, he ran across the tape again. Since he had nothing to do, he decided to watch the tape. On the tape was a sticky note that said, "Watch your right arm." As Edwin watched the tape of himself, he noticed every time he jumped a hurdle he would drop his right arm. This was an exciting discovery for him. He showed the tape to his coach, and they began to work on keeping the arm up as he jumped the hurdles. He worked at length on it in practice, but to no avail. His times actually got slower, as he concentrated on his arm. The Olympics were nearing, and his coach was getting very concerned. The coach suggested Edwin go back to the old way. But, in a final attempt, Edwin kept his right arm up. His time went down a couple of tenths of a second, and Edwin was on his way. He compiled a record that included four years of competition, more than a hundred meets, with zero losses. It was a small change that over time made a big difference.

Chapter 7
Personal Awareness

"Leaders learn most often from their experiences-especially their failures. Too often, though, they miss the lessons. They lack the reflective capacity to learn on their own..."

Lee Bolman and Terrence Deal - <u>Leading with Soul</u>

The rounded stones washed smooth by the winds and water of Lake Superior shifted beneath my feet. After ten days on the trail, the instructor would teach me one of the most important lessons that would come out of this experience. As she prepared to leave me for my 54-hour solo and fast, she began to open my eyes to all of the choices I had made and not made over the past ten days. In a brief moment, my security was dissolved and my soul was laid bare as I realized how unaware I was of my own experience.[1]

Process Facilitation is about learning to pay attention to the things that often go unnoticed. It requires the facilitator to possess certain attitudes and disciplines that were a part of our ancient wisdom but have been lost in twenty-first century America. Things such as a willingness to suspend certainty, silence and solitude are being rediscovered. Their greatest gift to us is that they help us pay attention. The title of this chapter is personal awareness. There is a dual purpose for personal awareness to a facilitator. It is an avenue for personal assessment for the facilitator, and it is also one of two areas in which the group members need to focus their attention.

Personal awareness is important to the facilitator for at least three reasons. First, the only real power a person has to produce change is to change oneself. It does not matter how much power, authority, charisma or charm a person has, he or she cannot make anyone else change. We spend enormous amounts of energy trying to change other people. What we reap from this fruitless sowing is frustration, fatigue and the belief that problems lie outside of ourselves. This has been driven home to us time and again since we became fathers. As we stand towering over our two-year-old daughters with everything in our favor—wisdom, power, money, size—we realize how powerless we are to really make them change anything. We can force our daughters to comply, but even at two years of age, they have minds of their own. We alienate others and disempower ourselves when our purpose in life is to change other people. The real power we have is to change ourselves. As a person becomes self-aware and acts upon his or her expanded choices, they will respond to others differently. If a person responds to others differently, he or she changes them unintentionally. If we change one part of the system, we can influence the whole. As we make different choices, our relationships change in response to those choices. The first step to changing ourselves is to become aware of our assumptions, values and beliefs.

The second reason personal awareness is important to a facilitator is that as a person becomes more aware of her inner process she limits her reactivity and expands her choices. If a person learns to listen to her thoughts and feelings, she increases her ability to live intentionally. As Chapter 5 discussed, much of our behavior is a knee-jerk reaction to the actions of other people. This reactivity keeps us locked in a cycle of limited, mostly automatic responses to life. There is very little sense of purpose or choice when we are caught in cycles of reaction. Thinking about playing a game of pool will help illustrate this point. Greg is not a very good pool player. However, he has learned to notice how unintentional poor pool players actually are. Watch a novice sometime. Novices focus all of their attention on the one ball they need to hit and are oblivious to the rest of the table. They hit the balls hard and hope something falls in the pocket. More often than not, they miss the shot and create a worse situation than they had before they took the shot. Compare that to good pool players who are aware of the entire table, not just the next ball. The shot they take is a choice. It is very intentional because they have learned what they do will have direct consequences on future shots. They are not at the mercy of luck. They help create the future they will have to play. The same is true for every one of us. As we begin to pay attention to ourselves and expand our choice of responses to our environment, we increase our freedom and our influence on our circumstances. The other side of this is if we are not aware, we force all those around us to live under the burden of our fears and vice versa.

The final reason personal awareness is important is that increased awareness strengthens a person's sense of identity. Continually answering the question, *Who am I?*, is foundational to developing an identity. Identity is what provides stability as we are constantly changing and growing. Identity ensures that though we mature and learn, the core of who we are remains stable. Identity is an anchor in a chaotic system. In a chaotic system, the changes and movement of the system are unpredictable. Responses are unpredictable but fall within certain boundaries. The anchor of identity acts as a boundary for the possibilities of our responses. Identity gives us security in that although we may not know for certain how new knowledge will affect us, we do not have to be afraid of learning something new. Our identity will keep us true to what we believe is important. The other side of the coin is, those people who lack strong identities often go from extreme to extreme because they do not know who they are, what they value or why they exist.

Silence of Unknowing

"Ignorance isn't caused by what we don't know. Ignorance results from what we think we know. Our judgments, conclusions and opinions about things block our receptiveness to anything new."[2] Much of what we do with personal awareness, as facilitators, is not about learning more, but unlearning what we think we know. Personal awareness is letting go of things that keep us from learning and living intentionally. It is a way of thinking systemically about our experience. Although most of this is unseen, our actions are created in relationship to our thoughts, feelings and beliefs. We focus primarily on the behavior. Later in this chapter, we will present a model for this systemic thinking called Emotional Chains. However, if the model is to be useful, we must understand the context in which this model is most effective. We mentioned earlier there are some attitudes and disciplines that will help us. These attitudes and disciplines alone do not make us more aware. What they do is create space for us to listen and learn. Briefly, these include a willingness to suspend certainty, silence and solitude.

The willingness to suspend certainty is about letting go of preconceived ideas and prejudices. It is a willingness to admit that our way of knowing is not the only way and our current understanding may not even be the best way. It is about letting go of our answer to listen for new possibilities. We will be able to practice this only as much as we are willing to believe that our value is a gift given to us when we are created. If I hang on to the belief that my worth is dependent on my having the right answers, I will only be defensive. I will never be able to let go. There will be too much at stake. However, every single person has value and importance. Those are innate qualities given to us by our Creator. If we think otherwise, we are destined to live fearfully.

Silence is about slowing down our busyness. Silence is not just about not talking. Silence involves intentionally removing all the things that distract us from what is going on inside. Silence means finding some time when there are no radios, televisions, friends or projects. Silence is an intentional pause until we can hear what is going on inside us and make some sense of it. What is it that we listen for in silence? We listen to feelings, to self-talk (those things we tell ourselves about ourselves) and to those ideas that we may think but would never say. In particular, we should listen for inner voices that tell us something about our worth, importance and acceptance. We believe that the most important of these is our emotions. Emotions are windows into our soul. Our emotions may be erratic and even irrational, but they do tell us something about what we believe to be true at the moment.

> **Silence is an intentional pause until we can hear what is going on inside us and make some sense of it.**

Solitude is the place where silence allows us to listen. Solitude does not have to be going out into the wilderness, but it could. Solitude is more of an attitude that says, for now, I must remove myself (at least my conscious thinking) from the normal, familiar circumstances and give my attention to something less noticeable but just as important as anything else that I am doing. Solitude can be found in a car ride to or from work. Solitude can be found at a picnic table in the park. When a person gets comfortable with creating solitude, it can be found anywhere, even in a crowded room. Solitude is about letting go of our restless grabbing for things while trying to satisfy ourselves. It is about being satisfied at the moment with what is going on inside. In solitude, we seek to understand, not to fix or remove anything. We simply want to listen to what is, believing that the rest of it will work out later.

Signs and Signals

Listening to our inner processes is not an easy thing. Even if we get past all the noise and distraction on the outside, we may find just as much noise on the inside. What is important to listen to? What are the signs that assumptions are operating that we may not be conscious of? There are certain things that we have come to listen to very closely. They are things that immediately grab our attention and make us question things further. We call them signs because they signal that something important has just taken place and we are reacting to it at some level. The inner responses that are the most significant for uncovering hidden assumptions are feelings of fear, anger and reluctance.

Anytime fear is present, something significant is occurring. On the surface, it may not appear to be significant, but we do not feel fear without a reason. At that moment, we perceive a threat to our well-being. The threat may or may not be an actual threat. However, if we perceive something or someone as a threat, then that is something to listen to since an assumption is active. The threat could be a fear for physical safety, or it could be a fear of losing something. Losing face, embarrassment, failure, loss of position, even security and certainty all make us feel fearful. As is often the case with emotions, describing this feeling or putting a name to it may not be easy. It could be as intense as panic or as subtle as just feeling uncomfortable. But if we will just listen to the emotion long enough to make some sense of it, we will generally find assumptions that we have not been aware of.

A very close cousin to fear is anger. Our most instinctual responses to threat are fight or flight. While fear tells us to run, anger tells us to fight. We have learned that anytime we get a sense of frustration boiling up within us, we should pay attention. Just as in the case of fear, when our reaction is anger, frustration, impatience or any other variance of the emotion, there is something occurring that is significant. All of these emotions usually trigger an automatic script we act out to reduce the effect of the emotion.

If we can learn to recognize our scripts and the assumptions behind them, then we can increase our choices for response.

The third inner response for facilitators to listen to when uncovering hidden assumptions is reluctance. Reluctance might be considered a variation of fear or anger; however, we think reluctance deserves some attention of its own. Reluctance is that sense of dread about doing something or seeing someone. It can be very subtle at times. It is often called procrastination and is seen as a character flaw. The flaw is that there is some assumption that causes us to perceive the event as a threat and we are not aware of it. We procrastinate because we lack the intention to listen to our feeling of reluctance and the emotional stamina to confront it. It may be the most devious of the three since it does not call us into action as fear and anger, but lulls us into inaction. Reluctance certainly creates more problems than it addresses.

Emotional Chains

Before we develop the Emotional Chain model, a brief introduction of the basic reflection model would be useful (see Figure 7.1). We begin the process with a shared experience. Our first step for reflecting is the collection of the raw data from the experience—*What?* In the *What?* stage, we talk about what happened, what we did, thought, felt and said. It is a fairly random recounting of the significant events that have just occurred. As members talk about the experience, certain patterns or lessons will begin to surface. These tend to be behavioral and procedural kinds of principles and lead us to the next stage in the model—*So What?* Armed with some new ideas of how to behave, members can then make specific plans to apply these behaviors in the current setting and hopefully in the real-life setting. This application occurs in the third stage—*Now What?* If we want to take this reflection a step further, we must be more intentional in our review of the concrete actions, and move our thinking beyond procedural principles and begin to pay attention to the more hidden components of emotion and belief.

If we are to increase personal awareness and intentionally pay attention to our inner processes, a guide would be helpful. The guide is called Emotional Chains, and it expands the simple *What? So What?*

Now What? reflection model already widely used in challenge course programs.

Using Emotional Chains is a process that allows us to think systemically about our choices and behavior by looking beyond the symptom (behavior) to the driving emotions and motivating beliefs. By beginning to see that our choices are derived from the interaction of behavior, emotions and beliefs, we are beginning to think at a level that allows us to move toward understanding. Sequentially mapping out our emotions, actions and reactions to a particular triggering event is the process of viewing Emotional Chains. It really does not matter if we begin first with the behavior or an emotion that follows a triggering event, but one should be chosen.

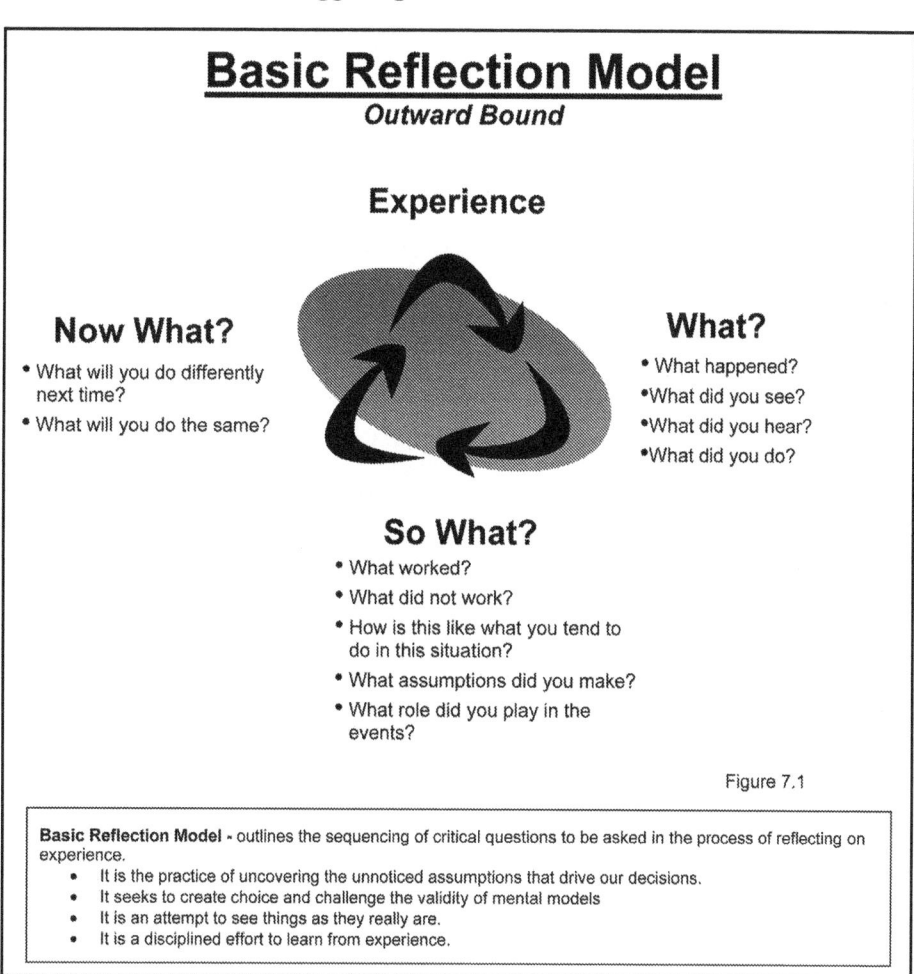

Basic Reflection Model
Outward Bound

Experience

Now What?
- What will you do differently next time?
- What will you do the same?

What?
- What happened?
- What did you see?
- What did you hear?
- What did you do?

So What?
- What worked?
- What did not work?
- How is this like what you tend to do in this situation?
- What assumptions did you make?
- What role did you play in the events?

Figure 7.1

Basic Reflection Model - outlines the sequencing of critical questions to be asked in the process of reflecting on experience.
- It is the practice of uncovering the unnoticed assumptions that drive our decisions.
- It seeks to create choice and challenge the validity of mental models
- It is an attempt to see things as they really are.
- It is a disciplined effort to learn from experience.

Let's say that we start with the first emotion we experience. What we are trying to create is a written map of the emotional and behavioral sequence that surrounds the trigger. After you have identified the first emotion, the next question is, What did you do in response to that emotion? If there is another person involved in the particular sequence you are mapping, then following the behavior question would be, What was the reaction of the other person or persons? These are the basic questions of the emotional chain. After identifying either your response or another's reaction to the emotion, you start over—What did I feel? What did I do in response to that feeling? This continues until you have mapped the episode. After you have created a sequential map of your experience, you can begin to ask questions that will help you recognize your beliefs: What belief or assumption motivated your choice? What did that behavior do for you? What did you get out of this particular behavior? What do you believe about yourself? We want to think about the most basic and fundamental assumptions at this point. After we have some idea about what assumptions we were operating from, we can compare these beliefs to see if they match reality, and we can brainstorm other responses we could choose in light of this new perspective.

An Example

For training purposes, we often use an exercise called Hold Your Breath. The exercise first begins with a person getting a baseline time for how long he can hold his breath. After that is established, the person is asked to hold his breath again. This time, when he is within fifteen seconds of his maximum time, a math problem or word jumble is given to him. The task is to work whatever problem is presented before taking another breath. The benefit of this activity is that it almost always elicits some kind of emotional response.

Here is how to map a typical Emotional Chain for this activity. The exercise is the trigger. The first response is to get busy. As the person begins to get short of breath, he begins to feel panic because time is running out. In response to the panic, the person works harder. As the oxygen continues to run out, it becomes difficult to concentrate. He recognizes that he will not finish so he quits. In response to quitting, the person feels frustrated. He begins to compare his accomplishments with others. Seeing that he did not do as well as others, he feels like a failure. By this point, we have enough of a map of the sequence to begin working with. We now begin a sequence of questions that will ultimately lead to core beliefs and assumptions. The sequence could be something similar to the following: (see Figure 7.2)

'Why did you feel frustrated?' *Answer*- because I did not finish.

'So what is it that you believe about yourself right now?' *Answer-* I am not good enough.

'So the assumption you are operating from is that you are only valuable if you can produce. Is that true? What are some other ways of seeing yourself in this situation?' (See Tools Section for a blank copy of Emotional Chains)

Conclusion

Reflection is very important. How else can a person slow down enough to ask the unasked questions? What must not be forgotten is that reflection is meant to inform us so that we can learn to make sense of processes as they are happening. If reflection is all that gets developed, we will spend all our time looking backward while the world is moving forward. Emotional Chains help move us forward and offer the opportunity to actualize relational awareness and emotional awareness. It is truly a systemic perspective. However, we can never just pay attention to ourselves, or pay attention only to the group. To clearly understand the dynamic processes of relationships, facilitators must be doing both. As we understand our own fears and assumptions, we become more open to encouraging collaborative relationships between others.

Emotional Chains Model

Triggering Event: *Hold Your Breath Activity*

- Gets Busy
- Feels Panic
- Works Harder
- Difficult to concentrate
- Quits
- Feels Frustrated
- Compares Experience
- Feels Like a Failure

Underlying Belief: *Only valuable if I can produce*

- Person's Emotion
- Person's Response

Figure 7.2

- Why did you feel frustrated?
  Answer- because I did not finish.

- So what is it that you believe about yourself right now?
  Answer- I am not good enough.

- So the assumption you are operating from is that you are only valuable if you can produce. Is that true?

- What are some other ways of seeing yourself in this situation?

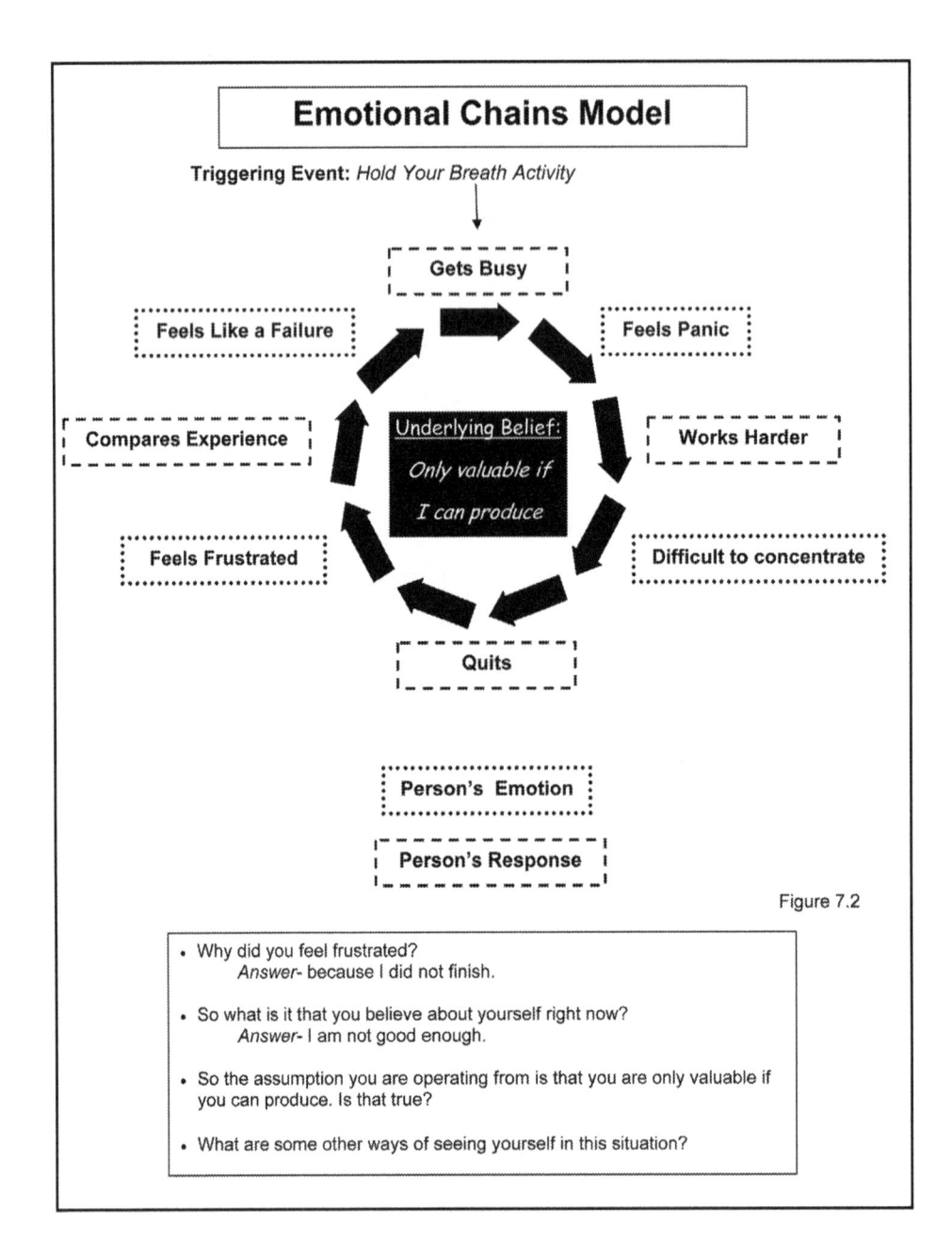

Chapter 8
Organizational Awareness

"Suppose we are able to share meanings freely without a compulsive urge to impose our view or to conform to those of others . . . would this not constitute a real revolution?"

David Bohm, *Physicist and writer*

The power of group process should move individuals beyond simply cooperating. We believe that the current trend in Western cultures toward groups and teams is an oversimplified concept of what makes a group. Simply putting several people together and encouraging them to cooperate is only the tip of the iceberg. To truly create groups with a sense of community, which leverage the diversity of their members, facilitators must help members change the way they perceive themselves in the world. Group process should help the group move from perceiving the world from an individualistic perspective to a mindset that truly allows the group to learn as a collective.

With this in mind, this chapter will present a way of looking at group process that encourages a group environment of learning collectively. This chapter describes what it will take for a team to develop the maturity necessary to change and grow rather than stagnate in fear. As is true with all of the areas of awareness, the lessons learned here inform the facilitator how to work with groups at a different level. This chapter also describes what facilitators should be passing on to group members to equip them to facilitate further learning themselves after the facilitator is gone. We want to take the basic reflection model that we talked about in the last chapter and expand it again to include collective reflection. By that, we do not mean individual reflection done in front of other people but reflection that gathers all the perceptions of group members to create a new understanding that could not have occurred in any single person. We will draw upon the research currently being done with dialogue to help guide us. In short, we want to learn to listen better and in a broader way. We hope that this developed listening will enable facilitators not only to listen to the content of group communication better but to also learn to pay attention to the process of the communication as it is happening. The power of group learning is that individuals only see part of the truth. Bias and self-preservation limit us all. Collective Learning is about a group reflecting the truth that an individual may perceive to others in the group, and thus creating a more complete understanding of the truth.

Elements of Dialogue

There are four basic elements the research identifies as being important to dialogue.[1] These are practices but resemble attitudes more than technique. The four elements are suspension of judgment, identification and suspension of assumptions, listening with new ears and inquiry and reflection.

Suspension of Judgment

We all have opinions about how things are. What we hear is based on these judgments or opinions about others, the world and ourselves. Suspension of judgment is not about *not* having judgments but about being aware that you are making judgments. It also involves letting go of certainty for a moment. Scott Peck talks about emptiness.[2] This is letting go of preconceived ideas, prejudices and particular answers long enough to consider new possibilities. Suspending judgment is simply a willingness to ponder the possibility that maybe you do not have a perfect understanding of everything. It is an intentional curiosity. Suspending judgment does not require things to always be black-and-white. It is a momentary expedition into the gray areas where creativity is possible. Suspension of judgment allows us to listen to one another and to really hear not only the words but also the spirit behind the words. It is a foundational attitude that lets us become explorers.

Identification and Suspension of Assumptions

This idea of identifying assumptions is a common thread throughout this book. Assumptions are those things we think we know. Individually, assumptions form our mental models, the pictures of how we believe the world works. Collectively, assumptions form those unwritten rules that become institutionalized as the culture of a group. What is meant by identifying and suspending assumptions is the practice of slowing the interactions of the group and somehow holding those interactions up in front of the group to reflect on what the group is assuming to be true. Later in the chapter, the expansion of our reflection model will provide a tool for exploring the collective assumptions of the group called the Team Interaction Map. We have found if we, as the facilitators, can map the interactions of the group members, we can provide a snapshot of their process that allows the group to consider and identify collective assumptions. We want to emphasize here that becoming aware of assumptions does not mean that we should not have assumptions. That would be impossible. It is being mindful that we do assume certain things to be true, but we are open to changing those if more understanding reveals the need. This practice also does not mean that everything the group assumes to be true is wrong and should be changed. Many assumptions are built upon partial understanding, but many assumptions are still accurate. What we propose is, if we can become aware of those assumptions in a real-time process and be unafraid to change those assumptions when it is appropriate, groups can act intentionally rather than being trapped in unconscious, reactive patterns that limit creativity and destroy trust.

> **Suspension of judgment is not about _not_ having judgments but about being aware that you are making judgments.**

Listening with New Ears

"Dialogue is not just talking with one another. More than speaking, it is a special way of listening to one another—listening without resistance…it is listening from a stand of being willing to be influenced."[3] Organizational awareness is basically an increased sensitivity to what is happening within the group. The primary emphasis is not about doing more or generating more talking, but rather about slowing down enough to learn to listen better. We want to make a few brief comments about listening that will help prepare our entrance into the arena of dialogue. There are three questions to focus on: How do we listen? To what do we listen? What will it require of me to listen "from the stand of being willing to be influenced"?

How do we listen?

Stephen Covey's book *Seven Habits of Highly Effective People* helped crystallize our thoughts about how we listen. For the most part, we listen not to learn from one another but for many other reasons that block learning more than help. We listen to confirm what we already believe. Try noticing how quickly you make your mind up about a person. Within a few moments of conversation, we either hear agreement with what we think or we hear points to dispute because they are different from ours. We hear what we want to hear. This selective listening creates situations in which we are simply listening for the next time we can talk instead of listening to what is really being said. That kind of listening silently degrades the trust and safety of the group. It creates competitive conversation, which is more about winning the point than promoting relationship. If dialogue is to work, group members must learn to listen and not just be silent while they prepare their next statement. In the end, listening with judgment will short-circuit the group process.

To what do we listen?

Learning to really listen requires us to learn to listen to more than just words. It is even learning to listen to more than words and body language. It is learning the process of communication. We must be listening to our inner conversations. We must also learn to listen for those things in groups that are often unnoticed, such as unwritten rules, defensive scripts and shared meaning. Organizational awareness helps us understand that just as individuals use defensive scripts in stressful situations, groups have their own defensive scripts. As group members listen together, they can begin to identify assumptions and values that create very binding, unwritten rules. These are those expectations that everyone 'knows' but no one ever talks about. When the stress is high and one of the unwritten rules is violated, the group reacts collectively in a knee-jerk response to help stabilize the group. Again, these kinds of unconscious processes limit a group's ability to learn and develop cohesion. If groups can identify some of these hidden assumptions and operational values and take responsibility to listen with openness, then there emerges the possibility of shared learning. This is a collective learning that is the shared perspectives of the group. It is not the idea of any one person but a group idea. It is an idea no one can really remember where it came from because it came from the multiple perspectives of the group.

<u>What does this listening require of me?</u>

Our society is segmented. We see ourselves as a collection of independent entities. This is what often limits us from truly experiencing community. If we are to create groups in which there is safety, support, trust, learning and creativity, we must reframe the way we perceive ourselves. It is not enough to stop at simple cooperation. This is a group effort, but it is a very fragile one. It is built on the idea that I will suspend my personal rights to help you for our better good. That sounds great. What could be the problem? The problem is that the willingness to help you is based on me getting something out of the deal. Do not misunderstand me; there is nothing wrong with helping others and getting a very positive experience for yourself. The problem with only simple cooperation is that we are still thinking as independent entities. Our groups will still be steeped in fragmentation. This is fragile because if cooperation becomes too difficult or scary, if the payoff for me does not seem worth it, we will back off and protect ourselves. Cooperation is only the first step.

If we are to truly dialogue, we must connect at a much deeper level with those around us. This connection does not have to be a touchy-feely kind of thing. Rather, it is the ability to quit seeing ourselves as so different from everyone else. It is the ability to recognize that there are more of our experiences that are similar than are different. The word we want to introduce as the next step beyond cooperation is compassion. Compassion recognizes that most of what we experience is common to us all. It recognizes that others feel the same things, hope for the same things and are frightened by the same things. Our competitive society has told us that to be important is proving how different we are from everyone else. Our society rewards the unique. However, those celebrated heroes rarely bring people together. What often create real definitions in relationships are disasters. A community is hit with a tornado, and everyone pulls together. Other disaster kinds of experiences bring out a deeper connection, such as fire, death and illnesses. What makes those times so meaningful is that, for a split second, the illusion of being separate retreats, and people see that their friends and neighbors are just like them. Our commonality, not our uniqueness, is what makes us significant.

As a group dialogues, the collective assumptions manifest themselves. Those things that were acting to suppress community are made aware so that cohesion, connection and solidarity are made possible. What is required to really listen to be influenced? The willingness to suspend our insistence on being different and to recognize the commonalties of being human.

Inquiry and Reflection

"Inquiry is about asking questions and holding an attitude of curiosity, opening the door for new insights."[4] As the fourth element of dialogue, inquiry is a fundamental attitude of being unafraid to let go and look for what has not been seen yet. We have talked about dialogue as a process of slowing down group interactions and holding that picture in front of the group so the members can examine the assumptions and values they are operating from. Inquiry is essential in this process because in it we do not demand that things get 'fixed.' Inquiry is simply asking the kinds of questions that allow the group to realize what is occurring. Inquiry embodies the mindset that allows the group to listen to be influenced. It is the difference between debriefing to learn and know one another, and debriefing just to get to the next thing. Inquiry does not demand one right answer. When confronted with a paradox (two seemingly contradictory things that both appear to be true), inquiry will not seek to choose sides but rather discover what truth can emerge from allowing both sides to exist. Most of us have been taught the lesson of inquiry but forget the learning as adults because Green Eggs and Ham does not enter our thinking much. If you want a good antithesis to inquiry, sit down and resurrect Dr. Seuss's treatise on inquiry:

> **As the fourth element of dialogue, inquiry is a fundamental attitude of being unafraid to let go and look for what has not been seen yet.**

"I do not like them in a house. I do not like them with a mouse. I do not like them here or there. I do not like them anywhere. I do not like green eggs and ham. I do not like them, Sam-I-am."[5]

How do you know unless you are willing to try them? How will you learn unless you ask and seek? Inquiry will take some courage. Uncertainty is not always pleasant. But to push through the uncertainty and truly learn something together will always be worth the risk.

Inquiry is the motivation that involves us in the process of dialogue. Reflection is the practice that creates the context in which dialogue can happen. "Reflection is about taking the time to observe more than one event and wonder about the connections between them, to formulate the questions that will take you to the next level."[6] To examine assumptions and to talk and think collectively, there must be space and patience. Speed destroys the process. When we get in a hurry, we begin to cut short the conversation. We subtly shift the focus from learning to finding the answer. An idea gets bypassed quickly; a voice goes unnoticed. Before you know it, the energy of the group is channeled into competing to be heard. Trust deteriorates, and we end up with a mutation of our conversation that takes the form of discussion, consensus or worse yet—debate. We must remember Collective Learning is about putting together the pieces to make a whole, while the other forms of communication that we have been taught are about breaking things apart. Reflection is the discipline that creates room for inquiry to take root and operate.

"And if you ask a thousand questions, yet do not pause to listen and reflect on what emerges in response, how will you learn?"[7] What does reflection look like in the group setting? Are we not already reflecting during our debriefs? Debriefing does provide a slot for reflection during the sequence of the day, but debriefing does not always result in true reflection. Reflection is more than just asking questions. Facilitators can support reflection by not overcrowding the sequence of the day. Pace is important. If trying to get to the next activity distracts the facilitator, reflection will not be allowed to occur. A good use of silence in the debriefing sessions operationalizes reflection. Silence is your ally in this process, not your enemy. Do not assume during long periods of silence that nothing is happening. Some of the most important work of the day will happen without words. One last way that we live out reflection is to ask the unasked. As we listen to what is being said, the door to hidden assumptions exists in the cracks between the lines, in the creases of what is not being said. The ability to think systemically or relationally will be helpful. When working with groups, take the time to notice who is not talking and what is not being said.

The Container

Our best guides in the process of dialogue talk about creating a container or context for dialogue. "David Bohm has compared dialogue to superconductivity. Electrons cooled to very low temperatures act more like a coherent whole than as separate parts. They flow around obstacles without colliding with one another, creating resistance and very high energy…Dialogue seeks to produce a 'cooler' shared environment, by refocusing the group's shared attention."[8] This cooling process will not likely occur unintentionally. The container must be created. This speaks loudly to the role of the facilitator and to what is most important. Trust, safety, honesty and acceptance cool the environment of the group. These are not easy attitudes to maintain when facing ambiguous and complex situations. The facilitator helps facilitate these attitudes by living them out and by believing in the process when the group cannot. There are times when the facilitator provides the will for the process until the group members can provide the will themselves.

Conclusion

Another way of thinking about how to create a container for Collective Learning borrows two terms from religious history—confession and forgiveness. They allow a group to maintain its safety and integrity in the midst of struggle. Confession ensures that the group is honest. Forgiveness ensures that the group members' honesty will not be held against them. Another way of saying this is unconditional acceptance. Learning is a messy process. It is often clumsy and awkward. The environment that will allow groups to flourish in this process is one where mistakes are not seen as failures but opportunities to begin again more intelligently. A forgiving spirit recognizes that everyone struggles and makes mistakes but that is not a reason for being removed from the group. The only thing that should remove someone from the group is that person's choice not to accept forgiveness and begin again.

Chapter 9
Signs of Hidden Assumptions

"We cannot change what we do until we change how we think, and we cannot change how we think until we change who we are."

Stephanie Pace Marshall, *Author*

We would like to pause for just a moment to frame this discussion. We find that, in learning, we can get caught in the details and forget why they are important. Up until this point, the discussion has focused on attitudes that create a healthy learning environment for a team. When such an environment exists, the team can learn collectively. By collectively, we mean the learning the team can do is more than the sum of the individual learning that is occurring. Learning collectively also means that a team can constantly change itself when necessary. Teams that seek to understand the connection between their behavior, their collective emotion and what the team assumes to be true are more adaptable and mobile. These teams are far less apt to fail because the open community of the team will seek to learn from setbacks rather than hide the setbacks. In the end, this type of team will be more resilient, resourceful and sustainable than a team that continues to look to the external environment for someone or something to blame for the team's current situation.

It is unrealistic to think that group members could explore their collective assumptions in all their discussions. Trying to practice dialogue in every situation would be cumbersome. There are some signs that a group is operating from hidden assumptions that are causing the group to be stuck and thus not learn. Before we provide a case study to demonstrate this style of debriefing, we will review the signs of hidden assumptions. It may be helpful to think of these signs in categories. We suggest there are two internal processes and group processes.

Internal Processes

There is much information to be gathered by listening to the internal conversations that occur when a person is in group situations. There are always multiple levels of communication going on. Learning to pay attention to these internal conversations can be the first step to identifying hidden assumptions. Some of the things that we find important include absolute statements, things that I think but will not say out loud and strong emotions. This tool for the facilitator is twofold. First, you need to listen internally yourself. Secondly, you can help groups learn by teaching them to pay attention to these three internal conversations.

Absolute statements are expressions that are founded in untested suspicions and simple linear cause-and-effect logic. Absolute statements are an attempt to immediately, with little if any discussion or experience, make a clear judgment about an idea, person or situation. These are common statements such as 'that won't work' or 'are you crazy?' The reason that these statements are so defeating is they are not supported by shared understanding or agreement. They are quick fixes to situations that seem complex and difficult.

In most conversations, there are always things that a person thinks but will not say out loud. Individuals should listen to the content of these thoughts, but more importantly, they should ask themselves the question, *Why won't I say them?* In answering the why question, we can learn about the most dangerous assumptions that are guiding the interactions. The reason a person will not speak his thoughts could be assumptions he is making about himself, the group or both. These assumptions could include thinking that he is not really that important, his ideas never work, this group will not listen or no one really cares. The important principle is that he is assuming the outcome without allowing the interaction to occur. This is very limiting and destroys trust. This attitude does not foster learning, change or growth.

We have already dealt with the final type of internal process that signals hidden assumptions, but we want to mention it again briefly. Emotions are the windows to our mental models. Emotions often shift wildly or are totally unfounded in reality, but they always reveal what a person believes at that moment. Again, strong emotions such as fear, anger and reluctance are the strongest signals.

Group Processes

As important as the internal signals of hidden assumptions are, these are often not made available to us as facilitators. Identifying the internal processes of others requires some level of honesty, vulnerability and skill on the part of the other person. These are often the very conditions that hidden assumptions limit. So the facilitator must ask the question, Are there external signs that hidden assumptions are in operation? The answer is yes. There are several group processes that tend to reveal hidden assumptions. These include conflict, members quitting, patterns of ineffective solutions, artificial rules and divisions, artificial complexity and incongruency between stated values and operative values.

Conflict is usually a sign that multiple assumptions are colliding. Conflict is not necessarily a bad thing. When different opinions are manifest, it is natural for some tension to arise. This tension can be the catalyst for real creativity. On the other hand, conflict is often unproductive. Conflict that blames, suppresses ideas or has at its core the conversion of others, is usually unproductive. By unproductive, we mean that it limits the group members' ability to learn from one another. Unproductive conflict is defensive. When this type of conflict is present, the facilitator should start asking those questions that will lead to discovering the real issue.

> *Conflict that blames, suppresses ideas or has at its core the conversion of others, is usually unproductive.*

Members giving up is another sign that something deeper is at work. This type of giving up is more than the choice to move on. We often see it when members just wander to the edge of the group during the middle of the activity. It is often the result of members feeling powerless and insignificant. It is our experience that groups do not purposely try to push members out. More often, it is an ineffective problem-solving process based on faulty assumptions. Before making personal judgments about apathetic group members, check out the assumptions of the group.

Patterns of ineffective solutions are one of the most frequently occurring signs. We are continually amazed that when faced with a complex situation and the need for a creative response, groups will most often just try to do what they have always done just a little bit better. The familiarity of an ineffective solution appears to be more attractive than the unknown creative solution. True innovation is the result of challenging what is 'known to be true.' When groups continue to try the same thing over and over again, the facilitator can help them become aware of this and challenge their assumptions.

We always find it interesting how collections of people create limits without ever being aware that they are creating limits. One way groups do this is by creating **artificial rules and divisions.** Watch the next time the rules are given for a particular element or initiative. What begins as three or four guidelines quickly becomes an extensive list of rules. The problem is that no one ever challenges the validity of the rules. Artificial rules are typically a result of one person's perception of the original rules. Artificial rules are often faulty leaps in logic. They are easy to avoid if the group is thinking together. More often than not, these perceptions of the rules are simply expressed and taken at face value. Challenging the statement would be much too threatening. That is, unless the group has developed a sense of trust that sees challenging perceptions as a way of caring for one another rather than diminishing each other. Another form of this same phenomenon is artificial division. Anytime subgroups are formed, it is automatically assumed they are teams competing for resources and information. The result is a tragic loss of collaboration and learning.

Another sign of hidden assumptions is **artificial complexity.** Artificial complexity is the habit of making things more difficult than necessary. The simplest solution is almost always the best. However, we live in a culture that has rewarded members for being different. A side effect of this competitive mindset is that there are many assumptions attached to elaborate plans. Sophisticated procedures or models are often associated with genius. The result is multitudes of complex theories that are of little value. They are impressive feats of intelligence, but simply are not practical. Groups tend to do the same thing. The hidden assumption is that the bigger and more difficult the solution, the better it must be. A facilitator should always challenge the 'bigger is better' line of thinking.

One final sign of hidden assumptions in group processes is a recognized **incongruency between what the group says its values are and the actions of the group.** There is always a gap between what people say they believe and value and what they actually put into practice. What the group actually executes could be called the operative values of the group. In the gap between what they say they value and what they actually do value is a door of possibility. What is it that is creating the inconsistency? Often times, the stated values of the group are things they feel they are supposed to value. Part of the problem is even though they would like to practice these values, their choices are guided by personal values and assumptions they are usually not aware of. If a facilitator can ask questions to reveal some of these hidden assumptions, the group can move toward creating a shared vision built upon values the group members believe in and not just what others say they should.

Team Interaction Mapping

In Chapter 7, we expanded the basic *What? So What? Now What?* reflection model to include the mapping of personal inner processes. This mapping technique of Emotional Chains allows a person to think about her choices in a systemic manner by understanding the relationship of behavior, emotion and belief. Becoming aware of this level of consciousness is empowering. No longer is a person held captive to simply react to situations; an element of choice is now available.

Just as individuals are held captive by these scripts they live out in response to stressful situations, groups and organizations seem to have their own collective scripts. Sometimes they are formalized into structures and policies; sometimes they are just as spontaneous as individual scripts. If we can empower people collectively to become aware of their culture (collective assumptions about how things should be), the likelihood of creating groups that are flexible and creative is greatly increased.

What we need to do is to take the *What? So What? Now What?* reflection model and expand it to the group collectively. This is more than the sum of the individual reactions and scripts. This process will open our eyes to the reactions of the entire system. We expand this model by making the *What?* stage a sequential mapping of the group's response to a triggering event. We want to map the important steps in the team's interaction. In the Team Interaction Map on the next page, those steps are what are recorded in the blocks. The facilitator should pay careful attention to the atmosphere of the group (collective emotion), the dialogue of the group and who was involved in these conversations. Another important piece to keep track of is information. How was information handled in the group? How was information generated, and how was it distributed? Finally, the facilitator can capture the level of participation. Who was active? Who was not? When were members active? How were they active?

With the sequence mapped, we can again begin asking the 'core issue' questions as we did with the basic reflection model. What are the assumptions and beliefs that are guiding the group? What values are coming to the surface? One thing that will be important to notice is, are there any inconsistencies between what the group members say they value and what they are actually doing? This will be a sign that looking a little deeper at such incongruities may uncover an unspoken assumption. After uncovering the core assumptions and values, we expand the *So What?* stage to look for patterns so the group can evaluate those assumptions and values to see if they align with reality. The group can also begin to identify structures, processes and policies that are really formalizations of a collective reactivity. Finally, in the *Now What?* stage, in addition to identifying what currently is, the group can identify new values, structures, policies and processes that are more compatible with the new shared vision of the group. As this shared vision grows and is passed on, it will solidify into a culture.

Case Study

It would be helpful at this point if we would move from the abstract discussion of concepts and look at a case that demonstrates what the collective reflection process looks like. The group was a class of undergraduates studying leadership that was the academic component of a larger student organization at an university. This group had a tradition of being a really quality organization that was effective but could not seem to "get over the hump." Students frequently waited until the last minute to complete projects. The advising professor wanted the students to become more responsible for the projects and organization and wanted them to become more collaborative.

The presenting problem (triggering event) was an activity called "Traffic Jam." The Team Interaction Map is a sketch of the sequence of the group's interaction around this activity. Initially, the problem did not seem too difficult. A number of attempts ended in failure. Participation was fairly high at this point. After several unsuccessful attempts, the level of frustration was rising. Many of the participants became much more passive. In the middle of the attempts, two group members came in late. None of the student participants described the problem to the newcomers or share with them what the group had tried until that point. The advising professor did inform one of the students who came in late. On the other side of the room, a small group, made up of the recognized leaders of this group of leaders, gathered together and solved the problem. They returned to the larger group but did not outline the solution for the group. They simply directed the members through the steps they needed to solve the problem. It was obvious that as this group's anxiety grew, the automatic response was for the formal leaders of the group to save the others. When this occurred, a strong reliance on hierarchy existed.

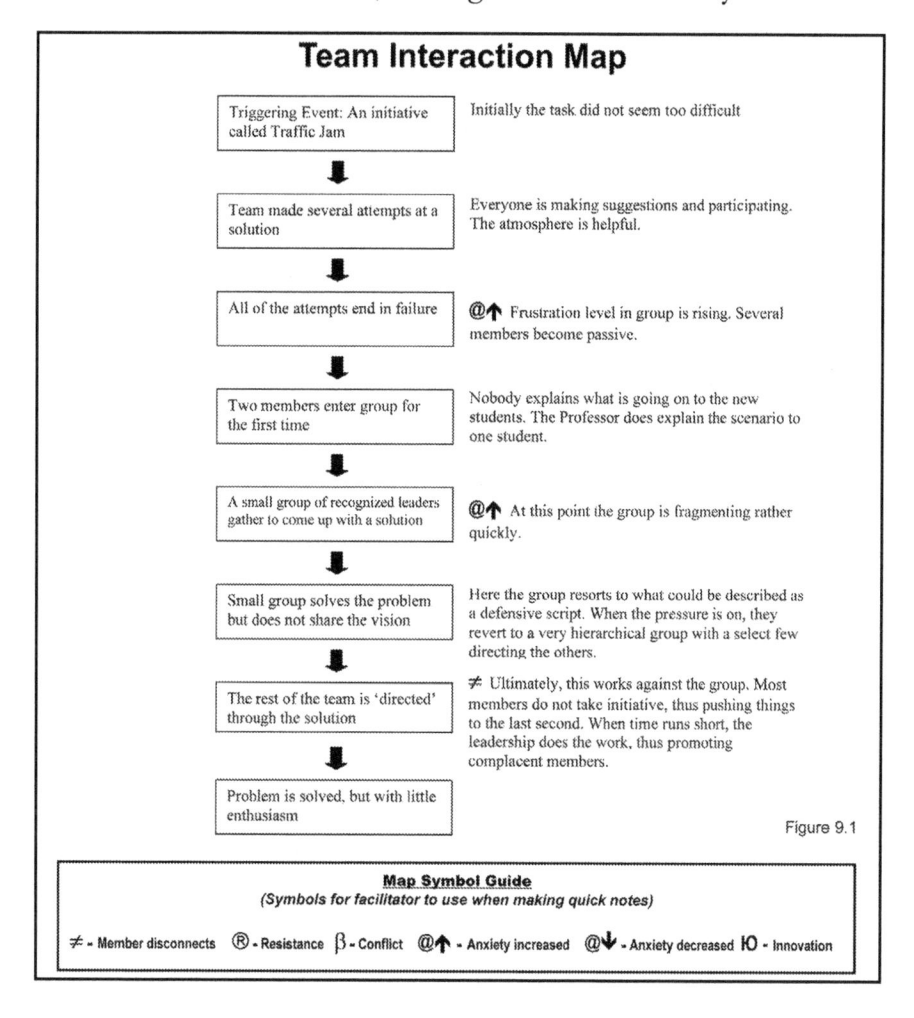

Team Interaction Map

Triggering Event: An initiative called Traffic Jam	Initially the task did not seem too difficult
Team made several attempts at a solution	Everyone is making suggestions and participating. The atmosphere is helpful.
All of the attempts end in failure	@↑ Frustration level in group is rising. Several members become passive.
Two members enter group for the first time	Nobody explains what is going on to the new students. The Professor does explain the scenario to one student.
A small group of recognized leaders gather to come up with a solution	@↑ At this point the group is fragmenting rather quickly.
Small group solves the problem but does not share the vision	Here the group resorts to what could be described as a defensive script. When the pressure is on, they revert to a very hierarchical group with a select few directing the others.
The rest of the team is 'directed' through the solution	≠ Ultimately, this works against the group. Most members do not take initiative, thus pushing things to the last second. When time runs short, the leadership does the work, thus promoting complacent members.
Problem is solved, but with little enthusiasm	

Figure 9.1

Map Symbol Guide
(Symbols for facilitator to use when making quick notes)

≠ - Member disconnects   ® - Resistance   β - Conflict   @↑ - Anxiety increased   @↓ - Anxiety decreased   IO - Innovation

After the exercise, the group was facilitated in a time of reflection upon the experience. The content of this discussion was typical of the *What? So What? Now What?* reflection model. The real-world challenge for the group was that team members often waited until the last second to do the work. There was little initiative except from the leaders. This caused the leadership to be concerned about who would carry on the organization after they graduated. When this interaction was highlighted in the form of the Team Interaction Map, it was obvious that the team was stuck in using an ineffective pattern in response to pressure. This team's preferred defensive script was to let the leadership save the day at the last moment. When the pressure grew, the team members would stop their collaborative process and revert to a rigid hierarchy (leaders taking charge). When the leaders took over, they stopped teaching the younger members how to lead. Ultimately, this worked against the group. Most members did not take initiative, thus pushing things to the last second. When time ran short, the leadership did the work and thus promoted complacent members. It was discovered that this defensive script was perpetuated by an identity dispute. Part of the group thought the purpose was to win the national competition. The other part believed the competition was a part of the group purpose, but the larger reason for being was to teach younger students how to lead so that they would be ready to assume leadership when their time came.

The final step of the collective reflection sequence was to focus on the necessary changes that would grow out of the new recognition. However, this group did not pursue collaborating on any new structures since the realization of this underlying assumption of identity was so new. It was enough that the mapping of the interaction sequence allowed the group to access the hidden assumptions and values that were informing their choices. The next step in the process would have been to continue the process of dialogue. As the dialogue developed, the group would have to create a shared vision of the identity of the organization. The group members would also have to identify structures, attitudes and policies that would support the new shared vision.

Conclusion

Organizational awareness is an application of the other awarenesses to group situations to identify and dispute the hidden assumptions of the group. The principles and practices of dialogue guide this process of becoming aware of the assumptions, beliefs, values and defensive scripts of the group. Ultimately, this is an attempt to generate Collective Learning. It is moving beyond personal reflection in front of others or even simple cooperation. Dialogue shifts the mindset of group members from me to we. It is premised on the understanding that no one individual has a perfect perception of the truth. The more a group allows its collective mind to work as an integrated whole, the greater the group's understanding of the truth will be. This is all built in and upon an atmosphere of trust.

Chapter 10
The Possibilities of Teams That Learn Collectively

"When we listen in the normal way, for what is right and what is wrong, then we won't be able to hear what is possible; what might be but is not yet."
John Elter, VP and Chief Engineer, Xerox, in <u>Solving Tough Problems</u>
by Adam Kahane

Often a good story is worth a thousand pages of theory. This is an attempt to describe what learning collectively looks like in the world, where, when one is pinched, it hurts.

Greg had the privilege of working with a team that seemed to innately embody what this book is about. This was a team of field technicians from a multibillion-dollar company. The team came into being as a result of a merger; thus, there were two cultures trying to become one. What was amazing was that this team had few if any of the elements generally associated with high-functioning teams. The team members usually worked alone. They were rarely together. Most of the interaction between team members occurred via telephone or radio. In fact, the two days Greg worked with them was the first time the entire team had been at the same place at the same time. He met this group of seventeen men and one woman on a challenge course one July morning.

The morning was filled with activities to help the group define itself, to help members get to know one another better and to form the group. After lunch, this team was given a major initiative to complete on a challenge course. The low element consisted of six different events connected in a continuous circuit. The entire element required some kind of traversing on cables. Normally, this project takes anywhere from an hour and a half to two and one-half hours to complete. On this day, this newly gathered team completed the entire project, including planning, in just less than sixty minutes. What enabled this team to perform so much better than the average? We suggest it was due to their ability to learn collectively.

At first glance, one would have noticed many of the normal characteristics of high-performing teams. There was a high level of trust, participation and motivation. However, many teams possess those characteristics and do not perform at such a high level. We should also mention that beyond these team members' efficiency what was so amazing was their ability to adapt. Their ability to change and learn seemed almost effortless. As Greg tried to identify what enabled them to do so, he noticed the following characteristics.

To begin with, information flowed freely and completely. Any number of team members played the role of spotter/coach. As one member transitioned from spotter/coach back to traversing, there never seemed to be a glitch. There were no turf issues, no power struggles. The information for successful crossings belonged to the team and was accessible to all and by all. The team had the ability to learn from experience on the fly. The resulting improvement was possible only because members were not required to start the learning process over each time a person crossed. All information gathered previously was freely given when needed.

A second characteristic that emerged from this team was the team members' ability to solve problems in innovative ways. All teams that participate on a challenge course are required to solve problems. What was different was the team's ability to solve problems quickly, collaboratively and creatively. Solutions came from all parts of the team. There were no designated problem-solvers, or chains of command. Whoever had an idea had the freedom to offer it, regardless of position. Not only did solutions originate from a variety of members, but the solutions made use of all resources. Many of the solutions the team devised required the team to use resources in a very different way than originally intended. It seemed second nature for this team to challenge assumptions, shift paradigms and creatively use all resources.

A third characteristic set this team apart from the rest. The team members used individual diversity as an opportunity and mechanism to improve performance. Normally, a team will find a procedure for crossing the elements and make it 'the way.' Most will be able to use the procedure successfully. Those who struggle are supported and encouraged but forced to use the procedure nonetheless. This team did not. Those who went before created a path and a way. What was so amazing about this group was when a team member came to that path but struggled, the team used that as an opportunity to ask the question, Is there a better way? Consequently, the team was able to adapt with ease. This adaptation carried no hidden cost. Often, teams will adapt a procedure to a member who needs help, but that team member must suffer the humiliation of failing on multiple occasions. The team adapts because a 'weaker' member forces the team to. This team did not require such a price. When a need to adapt was perceived, it happened without cost.

Now it may be this team just experienced a mysterious synergy. The planets were aligned, and all just fell into place. We are certainly not saying the team members performed at this level because they were purposely practicing Process Facilitation or that these observations were part of any scientific study. The purpose of this example is not to prove any theory. This example is merely a description. Teams can learn collectively when they do not force members to choose either the team or the individual. Both ends of that continuum are maintained. When teams do learn collectively, the results are absolutely magical. Thanks to this team of field hands. They provided a glimpse of what can be.

Tools

Team development requires more of a facilitator than being able to lead a group through a few exercises, no matter how good the activities are. Whereas activities can bring issues to the surface and can lead to new awareness, the development of the critical meta-skills for sustainable collective learning will require tools that help individuals, teams and leaders assess, track and explore the real world behavior that impacts the team's interaction. In the last section, we looked at four critical core abilities—emotional awareness, critical reflection, courage and systems thinking that are essential to new generation teams. These four core abilities when combined create two Meta-skills that equip individuals and teams to continue to grow and develop for the long haul. Emotional awareness and courage combine to form the Meta-skill we call Emotional Maturity. Critical reflection and systems thinking combine to create the Meta-skill Critical Thinking.

The following section contains tools that will help the facilitator assess, track and pinpoint habits and tendencies that may be limiting the team's effectiveness with these two Meta-skills.

TOOLS
- Meta-Skills of Collective Learning Dynamic
- Collaborative Leader Profile
- Meeting Interaction Assessment
- Emotional Chains
- The Emotional Shifts within the Collective Learning Dynamic
- Guided Learning Conversations
- Experiential Reflection Models
- Polarity Maps
- Action Learning Process
- Team Interaction Map
- Team Contribution Map
- Structured Observation Worksheet

Meta-Skills of **Collective Learning Dynamic**

Here are the two Meta-skills individuals and groups need to have – Emotional Maturity (Emotional Awareness and Courage) and Critical Thinking (Critical Reflection and Systems Thinking).

All of the following tools are organized around these two Meta-skills made up of the four core abilities. Recognize that in the real world there is not always a clean separation of the two Meta-skills. You may find a need to target one more than the other. You might have a group that is good at thinking systemically but they don't understand the emotional maturity side. When you use one you will be using the other also.

Emotional Maturity is the ability to monitor the emotional state of self and others, to regulate oneself in the face of anxiety rather than be reactive and to tolerate high levels of emotional discomfort. It is having the courage to do the right thing even though it is uncomfortable and making choices based on purpose and principle rather than fear or the need for control.

> **Emotional Awareness** involves the ability to monitor and manage the emotional atmosphere in the team and our own emotional state with the intent of reducing our reactivity to one another.
>
> **Courage** is the ability to be comfortable enough with discomfort to allow learning to take place.

Critical Thinking is the ability to become aware of our assumptions, see the interconnectedness of things and consistently reflect and learn from our experiences.

> **Critical Reflection** is the practice of uncovering the unnoticed assumptions that drive our decisions.

Systems Thinking is a way of looking at the world that sees the connectedness of things. When we think systemically we will see the mutual influence of all involved including our own contributions to whatever state or dynamics currently exist.

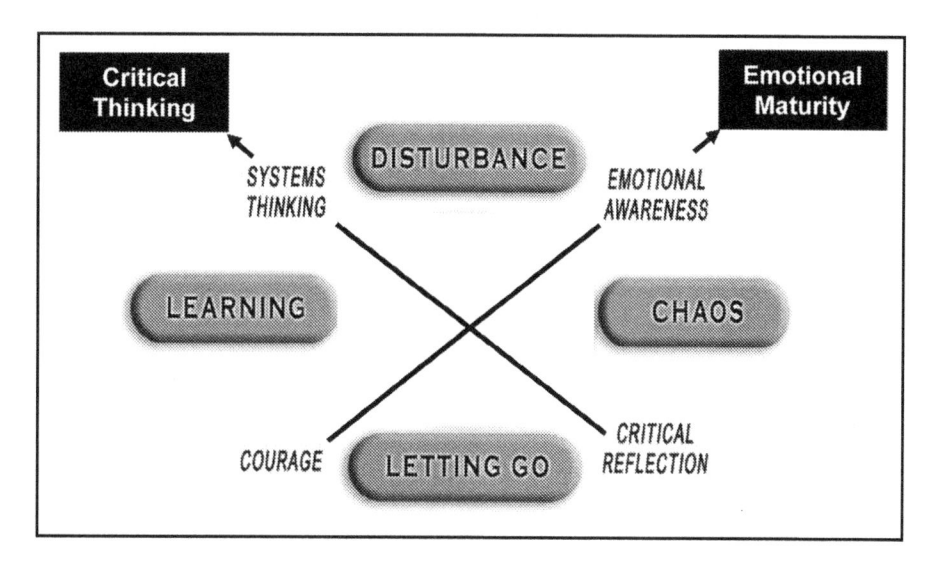

	Critical Thinking		Emotional Maturity
	SYSTEMS THINKING	DISTURBANCE	EMOTIONAL AWARENESS
	LEARNING		CHAOS
	COURAGE	LETTING GO	CRITICAL REFLECTION

Assessment

Tool: Collaborative Leader Profile

Purpose:
The more differentiated a leader becomes the greater their capacity for trust and collaboration. This increased capacity means they have less of a need for control and certainty.

The following assessment provides some questions to start thinking about the quality of your interactions with others. The goal of this assessment is to provide a starting point and then to watch for improvement. It is a life-long journey to become a more effective, differentiated leader.

Use these questions as a way to increase the perspective on your abilities and highlight areas for improvement.

Instructions:
Use the scale on the continuum after each question to rate the person's abilities. The scale runs from 1 to 7 with descriptions under each end of the continuum. Please use the entire scale to reflect your most accurate response and be as honest as possible.

The name you put on the assessment is the person for whom you are giving the feedback.

Your name will not be attached to your comments, just your position which will be labeled with other similar position responses.

While it is important to be thoughtful, don't agonize over each response. This assessment should not take more than 15 minutes. Please add your comments in the section after each question to explain the number you chose. This explanation will help provide context for the person in order for them to improve.

Facilitator Notes:

Remind people about Feedback Tips:

Be Behavior Specific - Give details about what specifically was done well or what might be done differently. Focus on behaviors that can be changed, not personal characteristics or interpretations.

Be Brief and Concise - Too much feedback can be overwhelming and isn't absorbed well. It's often reasonable to select the most important point or two, and leave the rest for another opportunity.

Be Honest – It can be difficult to provide constructive feedback. It is important to remember that by not providing honest observations, we limit the ability of others to learn, grow and improve.

The Collaborative Leader Profile

Name of person you are rating: Date: Your Role:

Write the number you choose in the Score box.

---

1. To what extent does he/she seek views different than his/her own views?

1   2   3   4   5   6   7

Avoids or ignores differences   Actively seeks out different perspectives

Score: ☐

Comments:

2. To what extent does he/she build upon or explore differences that are raised?

1   2   3   4   5   6   7

Quickly eliminates differences   Actively explores the perspectives and concerns of others

Score: ☐

Comments:

3. How does he/she respond when others question or disagree with his/her ideas?

1   2   3   4   5   6   7

Becomes defensive if others question his/her ideas   Actively seeks to understand the perspective of those who may disagree with him/her

Score: ☐

Comments:

4. When tension rises in a discussion, how does he/she respond? Do they seek a quick fix such as taking control and quashing the issue, withdraw, change the subject, use humor or give quick agreement to relieve the tension or do they acknowledge the tension and seek to understand the root issues behind it?

1   2   3   4   5   6   7

Quick fixes to restore comfort   Seeks out root causes of tension

Score: ☐

Comments:

© Greg Robinson Ph.D.

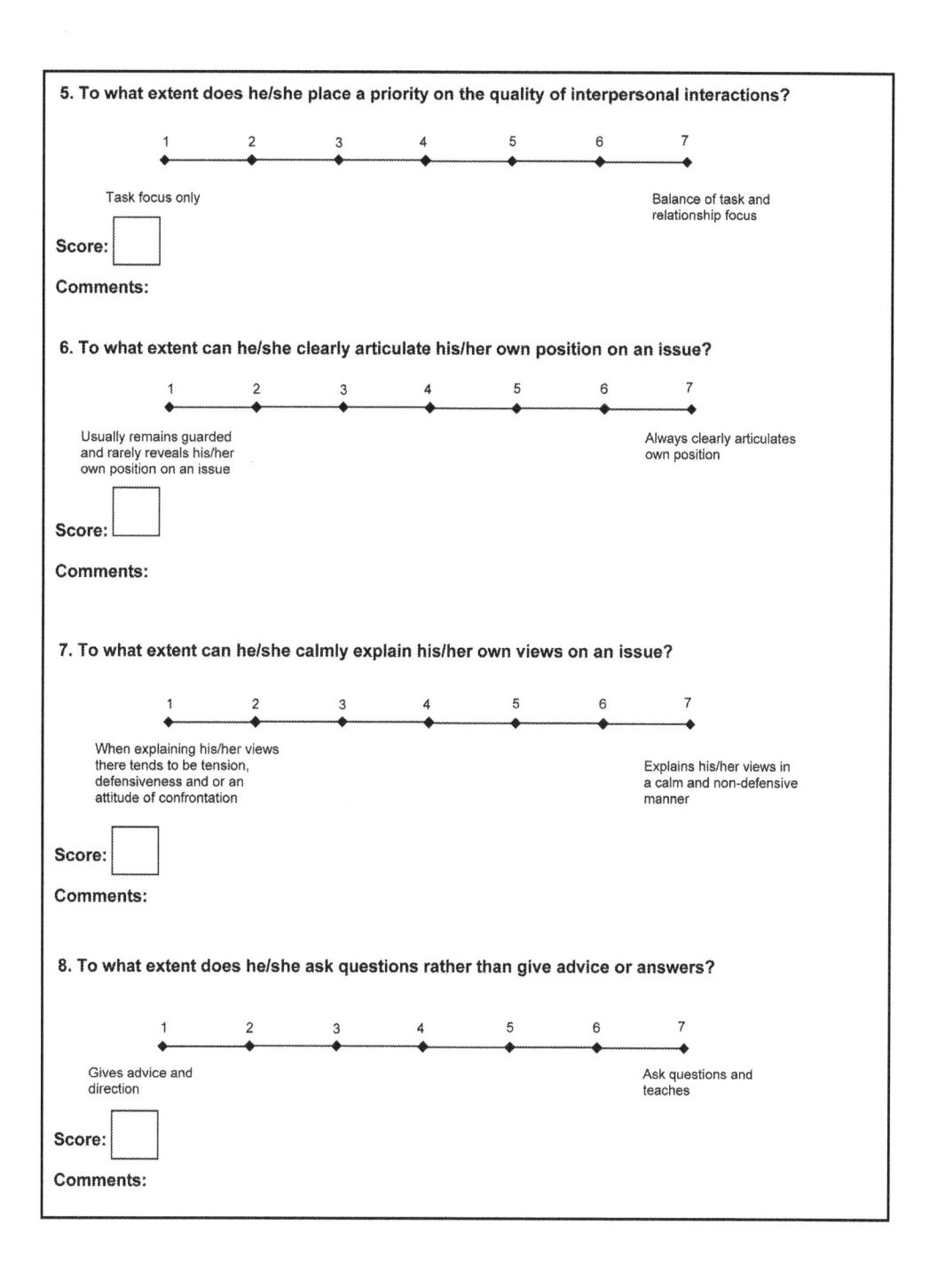

5. To what extent does he/she place a priority on the quality of interpersonal interactions?

1 — 2 — 3 — 4 — 5 — 6 — 7

Task focus only   Balance of task and
                                                     relationship focus

Score: ☐

Comments:

6. To what extent can he/she clearly articulate his/her own position on an issue?

1 — 2 — 3 — 4 — 5 — 6 — 7

Usually remains guarded   Always clearly articulates
and rarely reveals his/her   own position
own position on an issue

Score: ☐

Comments:

7. To what extent can he/she calmly explain his/her own views on an issue?

1 — 2 — 3 — 4 — 5 — 6 — 7

When explaining his/her views   Explains his/her views in
there tends to be tension,   a calm and non-defensive
defensiveness and or an   manner
attitude of confrontation

Score: ☐

Comments:

8. To what extent does he/she ask questions rather than give advice or answers?

1 — 2 — 3 — 4 — 5 — 6 — 7

Gives advice and   Ask questions and
direction   teaches

Score: ☐

Comments:

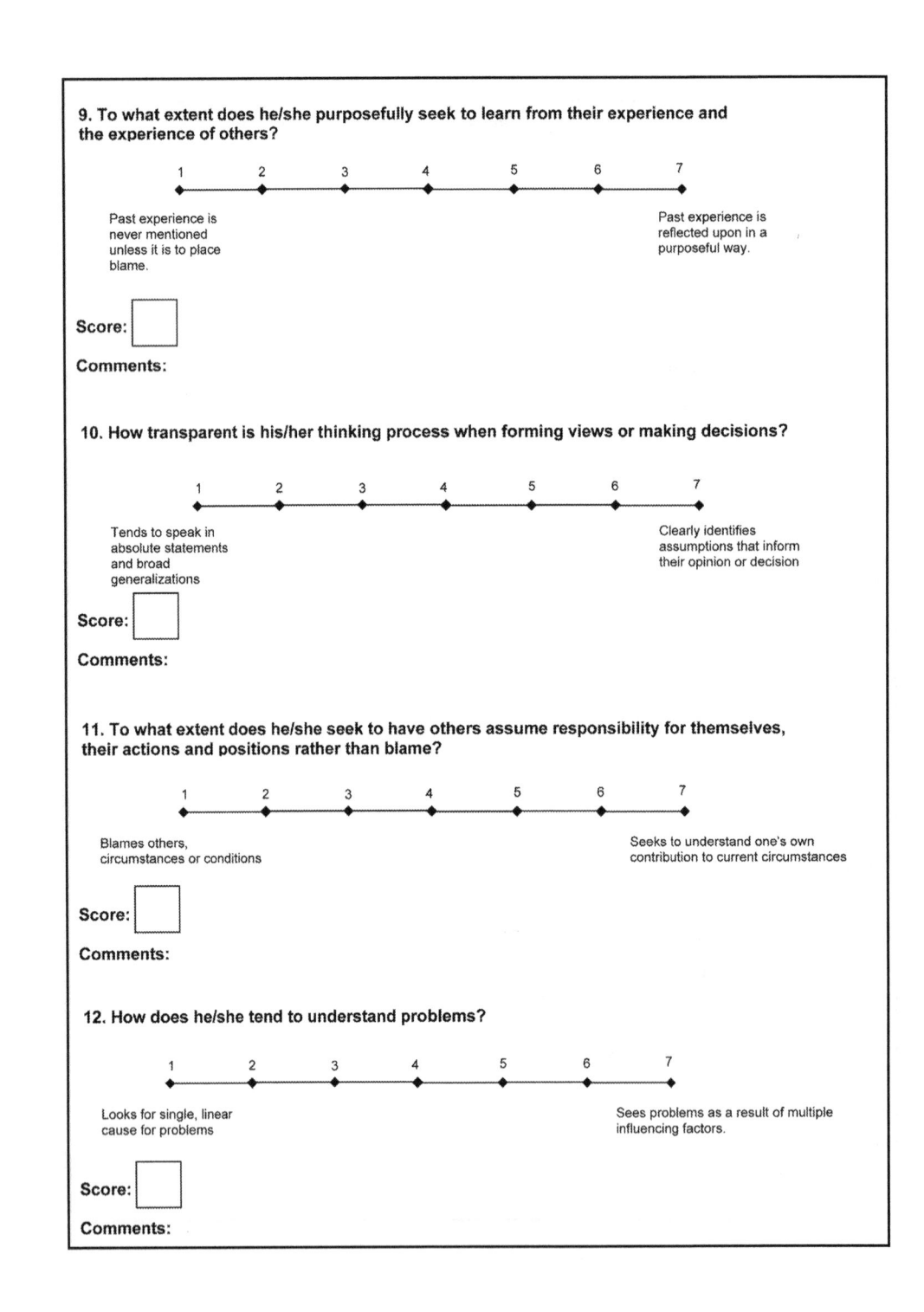

9. To what extent does he/she purposefully seek to learn from their experience and the experience of others?

1 — 2 — 3 — 4 — 5 — 6 — 7

Past experience is never mentioned unless it is to place blame.

Past experience is reflected upon in a purposeful way.

Score: ☐

Comments:

10. How transparent is his/her thinking process when forming views or making decisions?

1 — 2 — 3 — 4 — 5 — 6 — 7

Tends to speak in absolute statements and broad generalizations

Clearly identifies assumptions that inform their opinion or decision

Score: ☐

Comments:

11. To what extent does he/she seek to have others assume responsibility for themselves, their actions and positions rather than blame?

1 — 2 — 3 — 4 — 5 — 6 — 7

Blames others, circumstances or conditions

Seeks to understand one's own contribution to current circumstances

Score: ☐

Comments:

12. How does he/she tend to understand problems?

1 — 2 — 3 — 4 — 5 — 6 — 7

Looks for single, linear cause for problems

Sees problems as a result of multiple influencing factors.

Score: ☐

Comments:

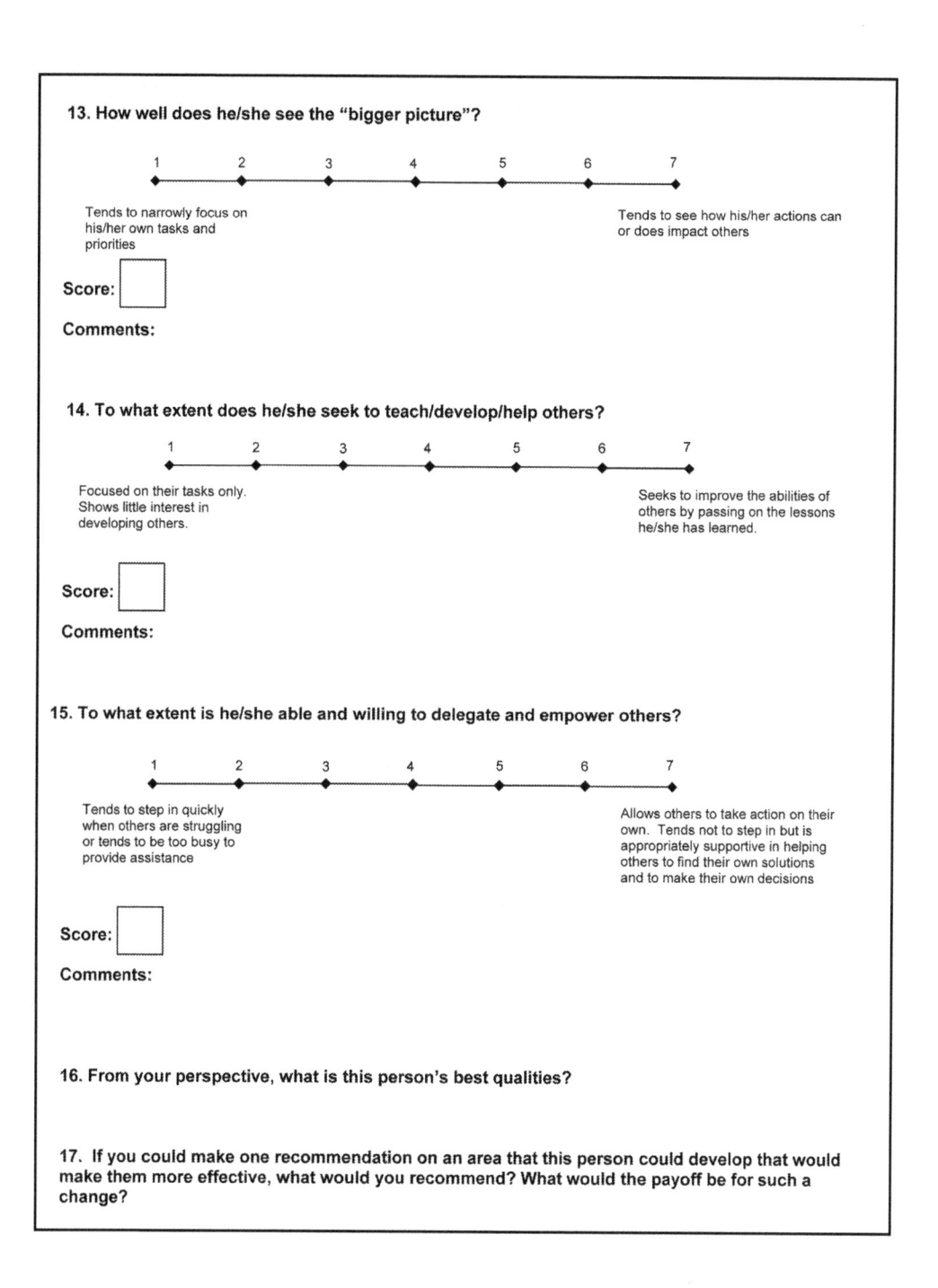

13. How well does he/she see the "bigger picture"?

1 — 2 — 3 — 4 — 5 — 6 — 7

Tends to narrowly focus on his/her own tasks and priorities

Tends to see how his/her actions can or does impact others

Score: ☐

Comments:

14. To what extent does he/she seek to teach/develop/help others?

1 — 2 — 3 — 4 — 5 — 6 — 7

Focused on their tasks only. Shows little interest in developing others.

Seeks to improve the abilities of others by passing on the lessons he/she has learned.

Score: ☐

Comments:

15. To what extent is he/she able and willing to delegate and empower others?

1 — 2 — 3 — 4 — 5 — 6 — 7

Tends to step in quickly when others are struggling or tends to be too busy to provide assistance

Allows others to take action on their own. Tends not to step in but is appropriately supportive in helping others to find their own solutions and to make their own decisions

Score: ☐

Comments:

16. From your perspective, what is this person's best qualities?

17. If you could make one recommendation on an area that this person could develop that would make them more effective, what would you recommend? What would the payoff be for such a change?

The Collaborative Leader Profile

Results

The composite scores on this assessment form are plotted on the continuum of 3 core abilities: Emotional Maturity, Critical Reflection, and Systems Thinking. These are three essential competencies for effective collaboration.

Emotional Maturity – the ability to monitor the emotional state of self and others, to regulate oneself in the face of anxiety rather than be reactive and to tolerate high levels of emotional discomfort. (Use the score from items 1,2,3,4,6,7 and plot the average)

1   2   3   4   5   6   7

Critical Reflection – the willingness and ability to learn from experience, to uncover and challenge one's assumptions and the willingness to ask questions rather than simply provide advice. (Use the score from items 8,9,10 and plot the average)

1   2   3   4   5   6   7

Systems Thinking – the ability to see the interdependencies between things, to see the bigger picture, to seek root causes rather than symptoms and the ability to change self rather than others. (Use the score from items 11,12,13 and plot the average)

1   2   3   4   5   6   7

The fourth critical competency focuses on the leader's willingness and ability to not only get work accomplished but to also facilitate the development of others. Organizations that have well developed leaders at all levels are more capable of responding to a changing environment.

Facilitative Leadership - the ability and willingness to focus on interpersonal process and the task at the same time, the ability and willingness to teach others and the willingness and ability to allow others to learn from doing without the leader being too close or too far away. (Use the score from items 5,14,15 and plot the average)

1   2   3   4   5   6   7

For a web-based version, go to www.challengequest.com

© Greg Robinson Ph.D.

Assessment

<u>Tool:</u> **Meeting Interaction Assessment**

<u>Purpose:</u>

The need for good decisions and effective collaboration are paramount for all teams but leadership teams in particular. The ability to plan, innovate, problem solve and make decisions is dependent upon the quality of the interaction among a team. Too many teams are undermined by emotional reactivity and simplistic thinking driven by expediency and the need for comfort. Meetings are an ideal place to assess the team's meta-skills since it is a specific place in time where habits and tendencies are most easily seen.

The following assessment provides some questions to help begin thinking about the quality of interaction with others. The goal of this assessment is to provide a starting point and then to watch for improvement. It is a long process to become a more effective, collaborative team.

Use these questions as a way to increase the perspective on your abilities and highlight areas for learning.

<u>Instructions:</u>

Use the scale on the continuum after each question to rate the tendencies of your team's interactions in meetings. The scale runs from 1 to 7 with descriptions under each end of the continuum. Please use the entire scale to reflect your most accurate response and be as honest as possible.

Your assessment and feedback should be related to the interaction of the identified team in the context of meetings in general and (specifically identified) meeting in particular.

Your name will not be attached to your comments. The results will be summarized for discussion and only the consultant will see the individual submissions.

While it is important to be thoughtful, don't agonize over each response. This Assessment should not take more than 15 minutes. Please add your comments in the section after each question to explain the number you chose. This explanation will help provide context for the team discussion.

Facilitator Notes:
Remind people about Feedback Tips:

Be Behavior Specific - Give details about what specifically was done well or what might be done differently. Focus on behaviors that can be changed, not personal characteristics or interpretations.

Be Brief and Concise - Too much feedback can be overwhelming and isn't absorbed well. It's often reasonable to select the most important point or two, and leave the rest for another opportunity.

Be Honest – It can be difficult to provide constructive feedback. It is important to remember that by not providing honest observations, we limit the ability of others to learn, grow and improve.

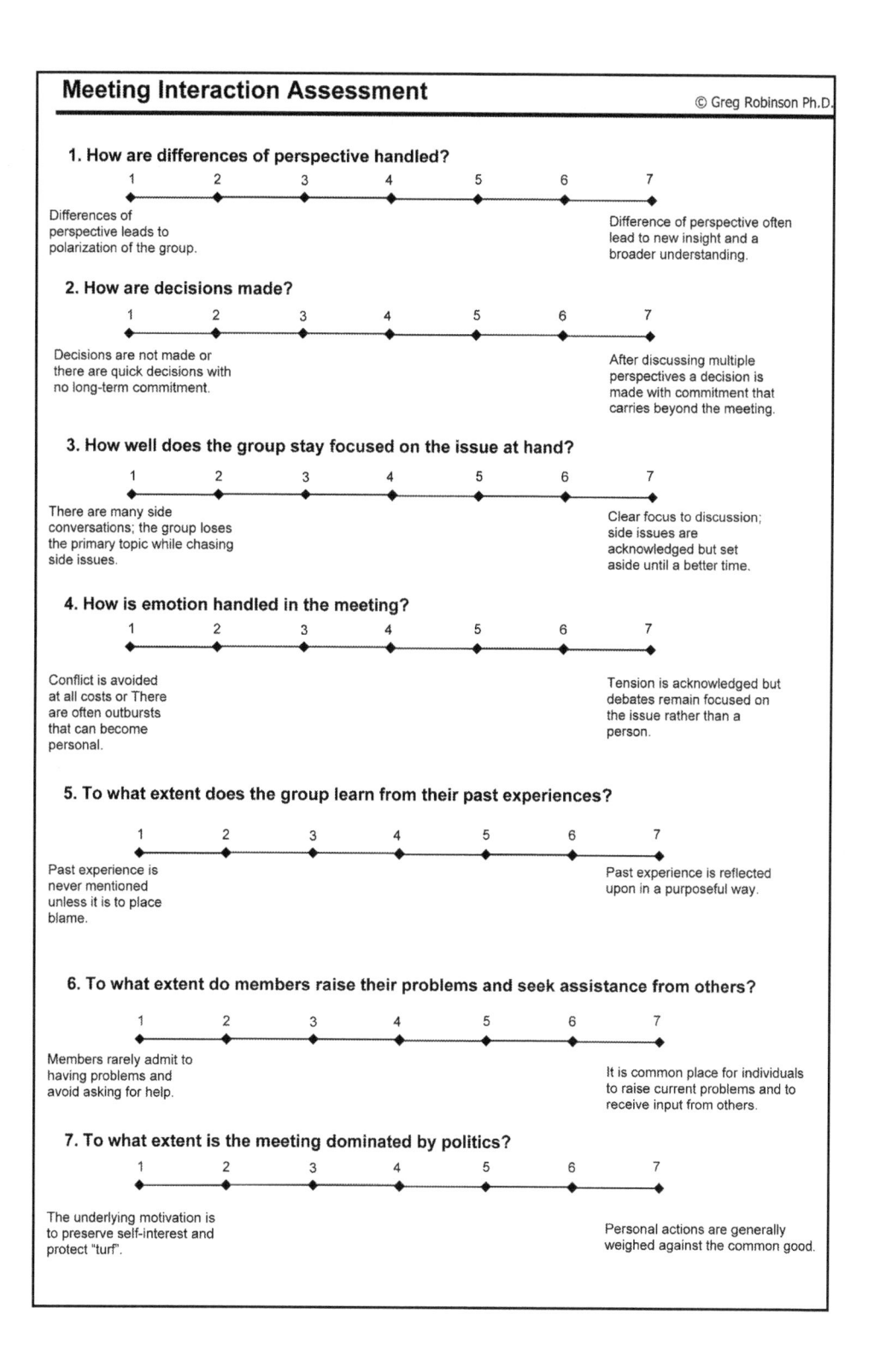

Meeting Interaction Assessment

© Greg Robinson Ph.D.

1. How are differences of perspective handled?

1 — 2 — 3 — 4 — 5 — 6 — 7

Differences of perspective leads to polarization of the group.

Difference of perspective often lead to new insight and a broader understanding.

2. How are decisions made?

1 — 2 — 3 — 4 — 5 — 6 — 7

Decisions are not made or there are quick decisions with no long-term commitment.

After discussing multiple perspectives a decision is made with commitment that carries beyond the meeting.

3. How well does the group stay focused on the issue at hand?

1 — 2 — 3 — 4 — 5 — 6 — 7

There are many side conversations; the group loses the primary topic while chasing side issues.

Clear focus to discussion; side issues are acknowledged but set aside until a better time.

4. How is emotion handled in the meeting?

1 — 2 — 3 — 4 — 5 — 6 — 7

Conflict is avoided at all costs or There are often outbursts that can become personal.

Tension is acknowledged but debates remain focused on the issue rather than a person.

5. To what extent does the group learn from their past experiences?

1 — 2 — 3 — 4 — 5 — 6 — 7

Past experience is never mentioned unless it is to place blame.

Past experience is reflected upon in a purposeful way.

6. To what extent do members raise their problems and seek assistance from others?

1 — 2 — 3 — 4 — 5 — 6 — 7

Members rarely admit to having problems and avoid asking for help.

It is common place for individuals to raise current problems and to receive input from others.

7. To what extent is the meeting dominated by politics?

1 — 2 — 3 — 4 — 5 — 6 — 7

The underlying motivation is to preserve self-interest and protect "turf".

Personal actions are generally weighed against the common good.

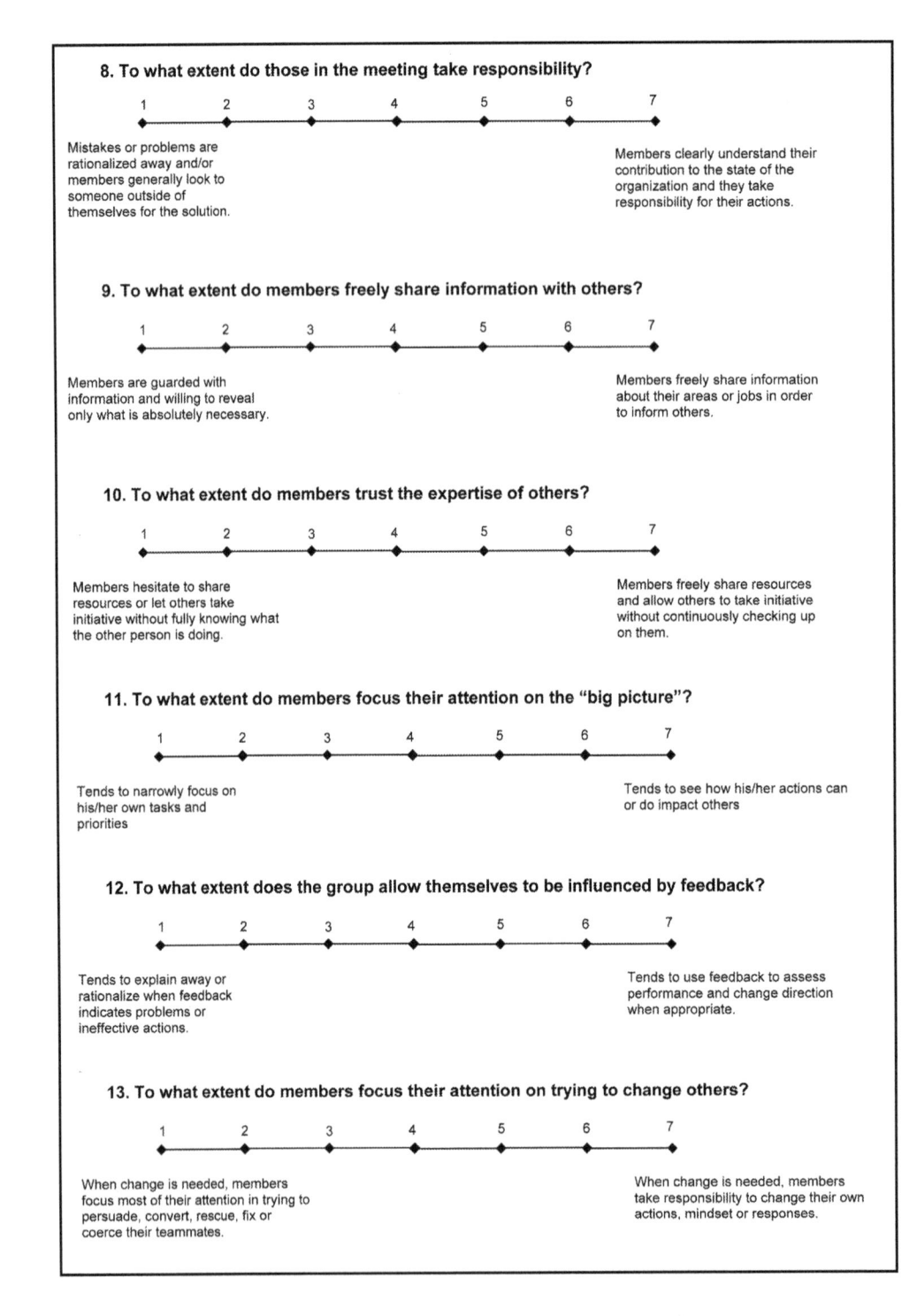

8. To what extent do those in the meeting take responsibility?

1   2   3   4   5   6   7

Mistakes or problems are rationalized away and/or members generally look to someone outside of themselves for the solution.	Members clearly understand their contribution to the state of the organization and they take responsibility for their actions.

9. To what extent do members freely share information with others?

1   2   3   4   5   6   7

Members are guarded with information and willing to reveal only what is absolutely necessary.	Members freely share information about their areas or jobs in order to inform others.

10. To what extent do members trust the expertise of others?

1   2   3   4   5   6   7

Members hesitate to share resources or let others take initiative without fully knowing what the other person is doing.	Members freely share resources and allow others to take initiative without continuously checking up on them.

11. To what extent do members focus their attention on the "big picture"?

1   2   3   4   5   6   7

Tends to narrowly focus on his/her own tasks and priorities	Tends to see how his/her actions can or do impact others

12. To what extent does the group allow themselves to be influenced by feedback?

1   2   3   4   5   6   7

Tends to explain away or rationalize when feedback indicates problems or ineffective actions.	Tends to use feedback to assess performance and change direction when appropriate.

13. To what extent do members focus their attention on trying to change others?

1   2   3   4   5   6   7

When change is needed, members focus most of their attention in trying to persuade, convert, rescue, fix or coerce their teammates.	When change is needed, members take responsibility to change their own actions, mindset or responses.

Results

The composite scores on this assessment form are plotted on the continuum of 3 core abilities: Emotional Maturity, Critical Reflection, and Systems Thinking. These are three essential competencies for effective collaboration.

Emotional Maturity – the ability to monitor the emotional state of self and others, to regulate oneself in the face of anxiety rather than be reactive and to tolerate high levels of emotional discomfort. (Use the score from items 1,3,4,8 and plot the average)

1   2   3   4   5   6   7

Critical Reflection – the willingness and ability to learn from experience, to uncover and challenge one's assumptions and the willingness to ask questions rather than simply provide advice. (Use the score from items 2,5,12 and plot the average)

1   2   3   4   5   6   7

Systems Thinking – the ability to see the interdependencies between things, to see the bigger picture, to seek root causes rather than symptoms and the ability to change self rather than others. (Use the score from items 11,13 and plot the average)

1   2   3   4   5   6   7

The fourth critical competency focuses on the group's willingness and ability to not only get work accomplished but to truly collaborate with others. Organizations that have well developed leaders at all levels are more capable of responding to a changing environment.

Collaboration - the ability to remain open so that all parties discover new ideas that they could not have discovered individually. It is made up of two factors: the level of trust and the need for autonomy. **Trust** refers to the willingness to be vulnerable or dependent upon the actions of others. Autonomy refers to the need to be in control of information, resources and/or act unilaterally from others. (Use the score from items 6,7,9,10 and plot the average)

1   2   3   4   5   6   7

For a sample report, go to www.challengequest.com

Emotional Maturity

<u>Tool</u>: **Emotional Chains**

<u>Purpose:</u>

This is a mapping tool that enables an individual or team to take a critical incident and slow it down into a single page diagram for reflection. The key is to explore the impact emotions, thoughts and actions have on one another.

<u>Instructions:</u>
1. Identify the triggering event that initiates the cycle.
2. Identify the emotion that you experienced first.
3. Describe your response to feeling that emotion.
4. Describe the reaction of the other party or the consequence of your response.
5. Continue steps 2-4 until the cycle begins to repeat itself.
6. With the cycle mapped, ask some of the following questions:
   - What is my behavior getting me?
   - What am I believing about myself?
   - What am I believing about the other person?

<u>Facilitator Notes:</u>
- The map is complete when the reactions and responses begin to become repetitive.
- Although the cycle may be broken by changing any step in the cycle, it will only be changed in a sustainable fashion when the underlying assumptions that promote certain emotions and behaviors are surfaced and challenged.

Emotional Chains Model

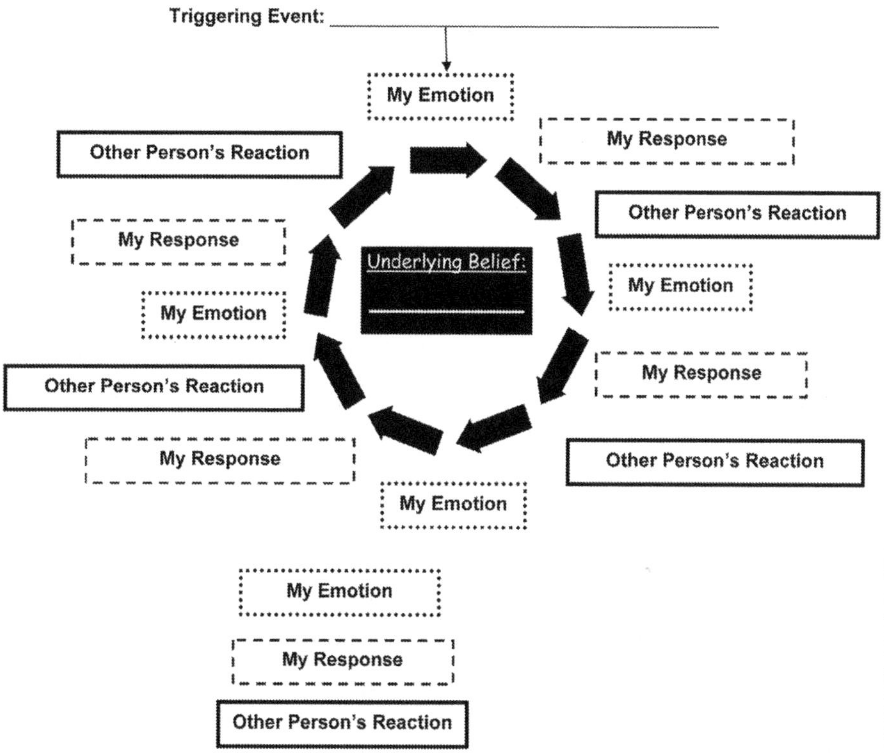
Triggering Event: ______
My Emotion
My Response
Other Person's Reaction
My Emotion
My Response
Other Person's Reaction
My Emotion
My Response
Other Person's Reaction
My Emotion
My Response
Other Person's Reaction
Underlying Belief:
My Emotion
My Response
Other Person's Reaction

1. Identify the triggering event that initiates the cycle.
2. Identify the emotion that you experience first.
3. Describe your response to feeling that emotion.
4. Describe the reaction of the other person or the consequence of your response.
5. Continue steps 2 – 4 until the cycle begins to repeat itself.
6. With the cycle mapped, ask some of the following questions:
    a. What is my behavior getting me?
    b. What do I believe about myself?
    c. What do I believe about the other person?

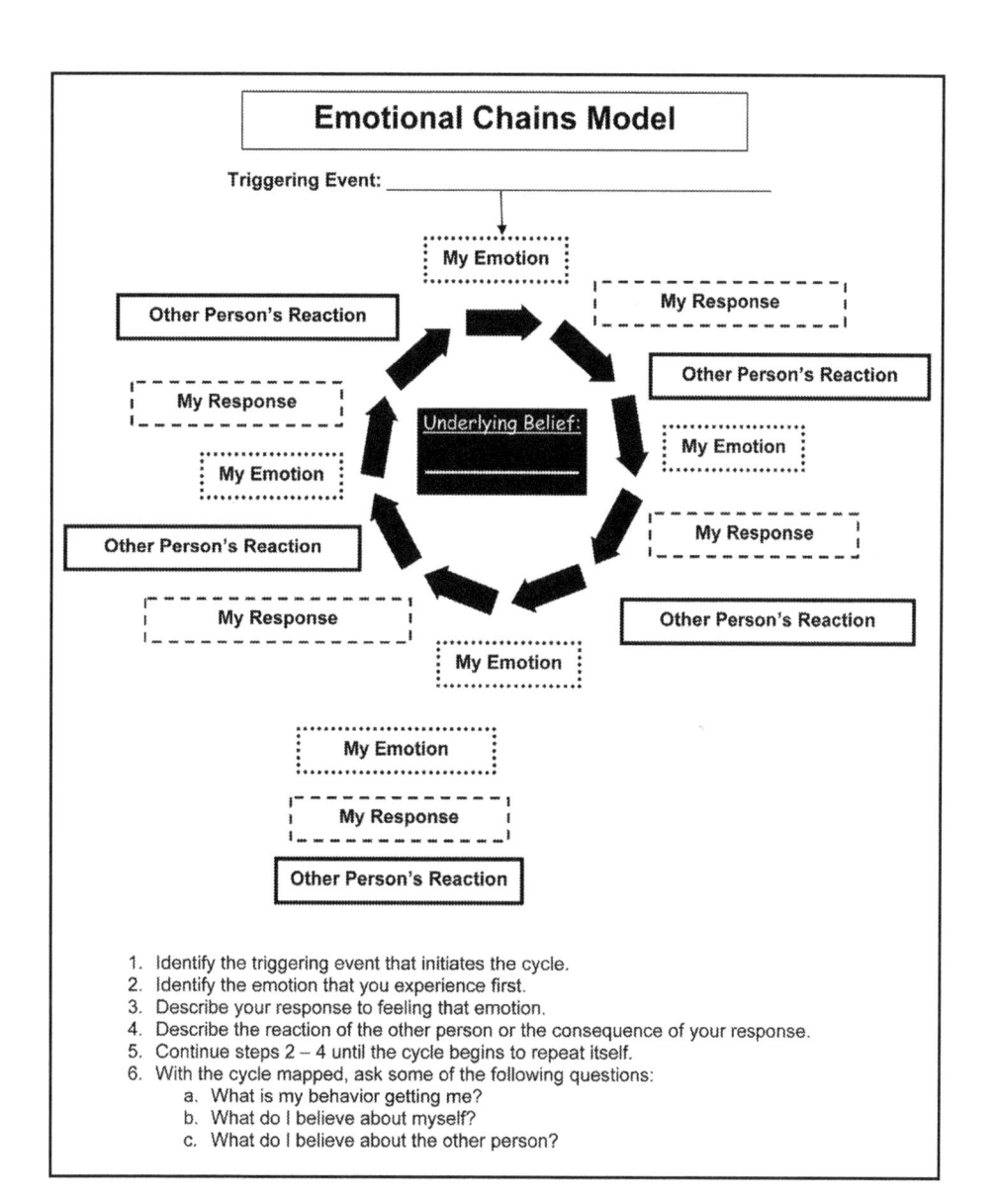

Emotional Awareness

Tool: The Emotional Shifts within the Collective Learning Dynamic

Purpose:

The process of differentiation(defining self) first requires an emotional shift if we are to overcome our fear. It is our ability to manage our anxiety that will determine if we become more differentiated. Differentiation requires asking tough questions, not rushing to solutions in tense and uncomfortable situations and the ability to engage situations that make us anxious rather than avoid them. This shift will allow us to ask different questions and thus find different answers. Unfortunately, the emotional maturity process is often difficult to develop. The learning wheel is a model that provides opportunities to make such an emotional shift and this version of the model outlines the type of choices that need to be made at each stage. Retreating from any of these opportunities keeps us trapped in our need for comfort and inhibits our ability to mature. This model is a useful teaching tool to help teams understand the risks necessary to grow together. It also, provides a roadmap for facilitators to assess what is the team afraid of and consequently may be avoiding. Are they afraid of becoming aware of the need to change? Are they avoiding the insight that might point out the need to take more responsibility for their own functioning? Are they simply uncomfortable with being open and vulnerable with each other? Understanding the potential pitfalls can help the facilitator or team find a way out of the a situation in which the team is stuck and not able to move forward.

Instructions:

Use this as a teaching tool to help participants understand the basic changes one must be willing to entertain in order to learn and mature.

Opportunity 1
Risk Awareness

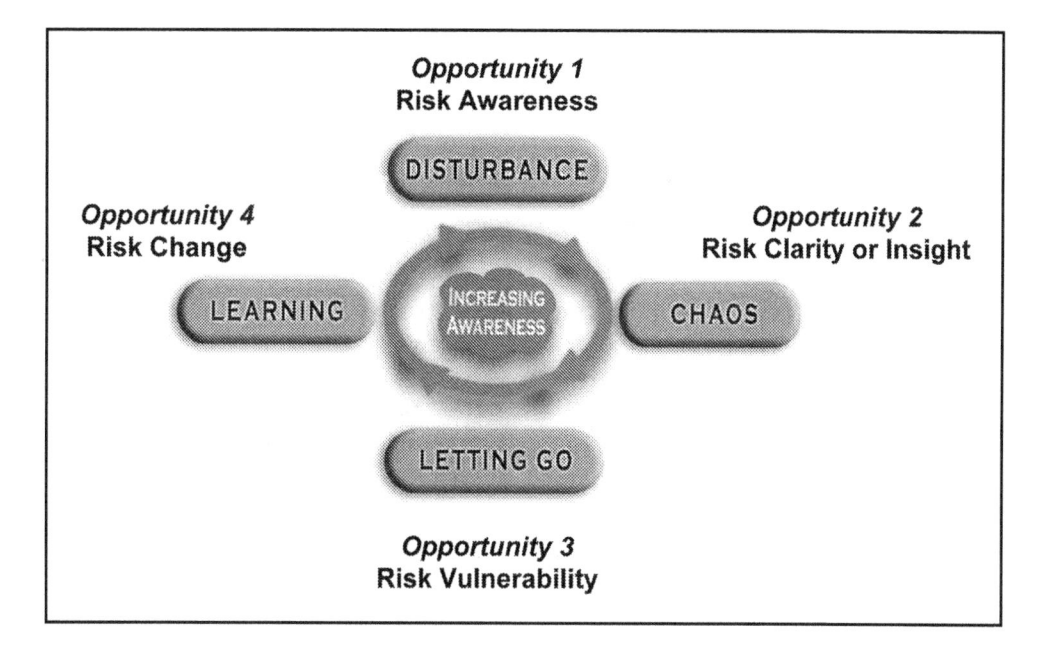

DISTURBANCE

Opportunity 4
Risk Change

LEARNING

INCREASING AWARENESS

CHAOS

Opportunity 2
Risk Clarity or Insight

LETTING GO

Opportunity 3
Risk Vulnerability

Critical Thinking

Tool: Guided Learning Conversations

Purpose:

An important way to learn to see the emotional and learning dynamics at work is to use the learning wheel framework as a guide to reflect on experience. There are two steps to mastering these concepts. First, there is the development of self-awareness, i.e. the ability of an individual to monitor their own internal dynamics in terms of emotion and thinking. The second, is other awareness, i.e. learning to observe others and use a model to make sense of what is being observed. This tool includes a series of questions, aligned to the learning wheel which can be used to guide reflection on experience. There is one for self and one for other awareness.

Instructions:
- Identify an experience that needs to be more clearly understood.
- Start at the Disturbance point of the model (top center). Move around the circle clockwise.
- Ask or discuss the questions in each box which are associated with each phase of the learning dynamics model.

Developing Self-Awareness

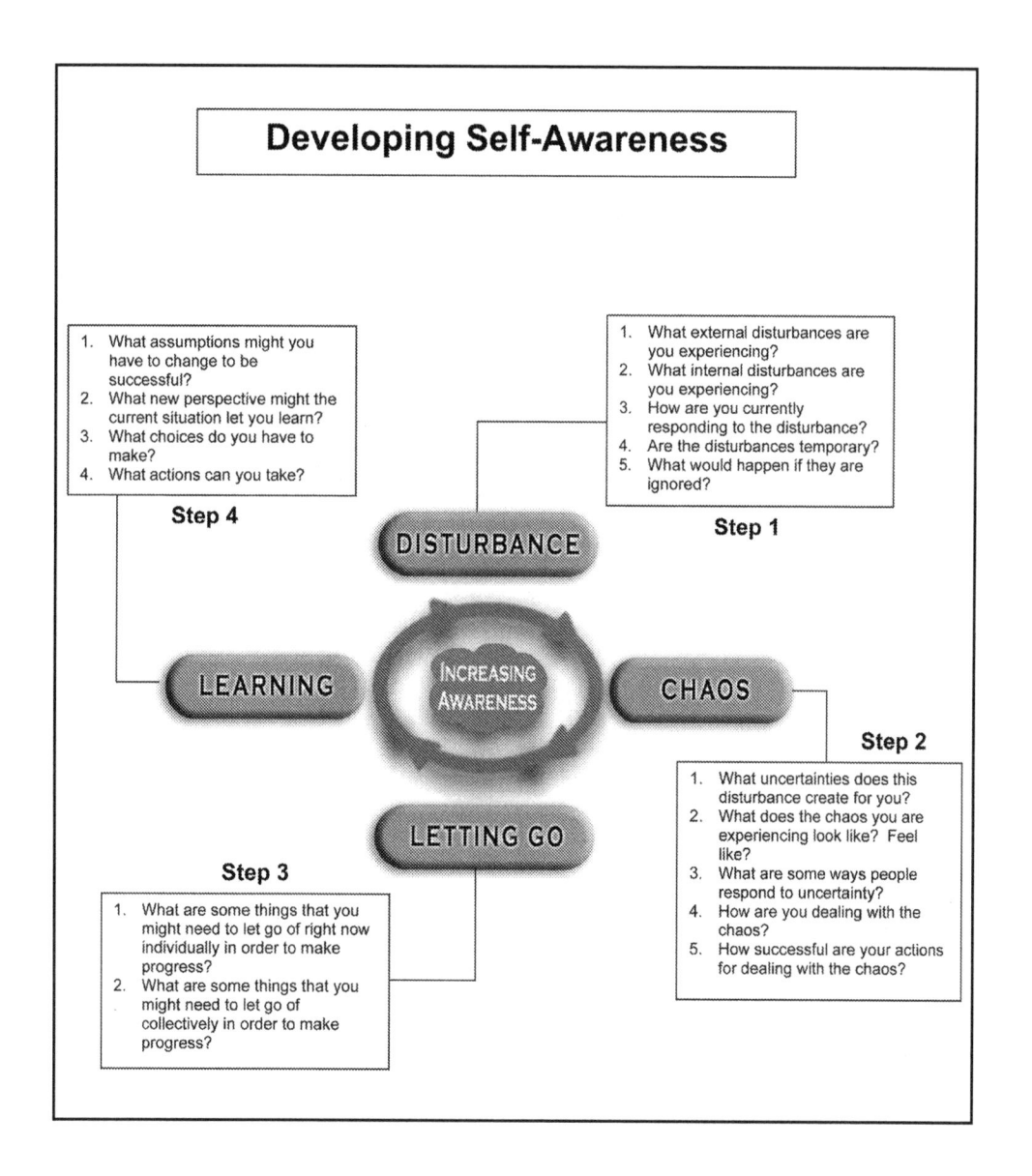

Step 4

1. What assumptions might you have to change to be successful?
2. What new perspective might the current situation let you learn?
3. What choices do you have to make?
4. What actions can you take?

Step 1

1. What external disturbances are you experiencing?
2. What internal disturbances are you experiencing?
3. How are you currently responding to the disturbance?
4. Are the disturbances temporary?
5. What would happen if they are ignored?

DISTURBANCE

LEARNING

Increasing Awareness

CHAOS

LETTING GO

Step 2

1. What uncertainties does this disturbance create for you?
2. What does the chaos you are experiencing look like? Feel like?
3. What are some ways people respond to uncertainty?
4. How are you dealing with the chaos?
5. How successful are your actions for dealing with the chaos?

Step 3

1. What are some things that you might need to let go of right now individually in order to make progress?
2. What are some things that you might need to let go of collectively in order to make progress?

Developing Awareness of Others

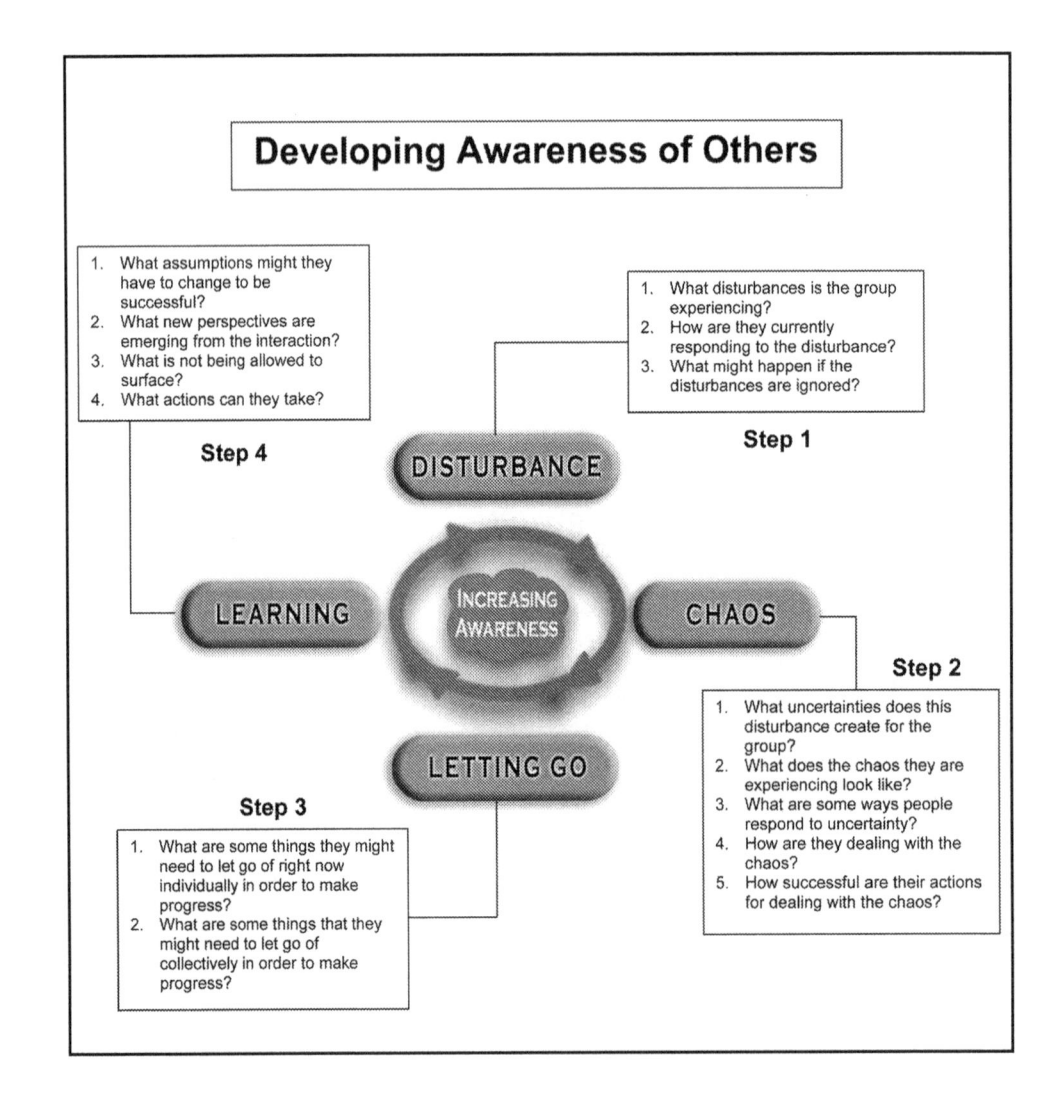

Step 1
1. What disturbances is the group experiencing?
2. How are they currently responding to the disturbance?
3. What might happen if the disturbances are ignored?

Step 4
1. What assumptions might they have to change to be successful?
2. What new perspectives are emerging from the interaction?
3. What is not being allowed to surface?
4. What actions can they take?

Step 2
1. What uncertainties does this disturbance create for the group?
2. What does the chaos they are experiencing look like?
3. What are some ways people respond to uncertainty?
4. How are they dealing with the chaos?
5. How successful are their actions for dealing with the chaos?

Step 3
1. What are some things they might need to let go of right now individually in order to make progress?
2. What are some things that they might need to let go of collectively in order to make progress?

DISTURBANCE → CHAOS → LETTING GO → LEARNING

INCREASING AWARENESS

Critical Thinking

<u>Tool:</u> **Experiential Reflection Models**

<u>Purpose:</u>

Often there is a need to reflect on experiences in order to uncover hidden assumptions, critical actions and new strategies for improvement. Unlike the previous reflection model, this model is more generic. It is designed to gather varied and wide ranging insights from an experience. The first example is the basic reflection sequence which is an established tool from Gestalt therapy. It is really a very basic, practical, quick look at an experience. The second example adds depth to the model by including critical reflection questions that seek to get beneath the surface of the experience to the assumptions and emotional process that influenced the behaviors in the experience.

<u>Instructions:</u>
- Identify an experience to be reflected upon.
- Start by asking open ended questions that seek to uncover **What?** happened in the experience. Once things begin to be repeated, then it is time to move on to the second stage.
- Once the important details of the experience are known, begin asking open-ended questions that explore the **So What?** or lessons of the experience. This is the stage to look beyond the outward actions and ask questions that seek to uncover the hidden assumptions of the team. Notice not only what they did but also what they did not do or talk about.
- Finally, ask questions that look at the **Now What?** or application of the lessons in new or different settings.

<u>Facilitator Notes:</u>
- Questions that change the pace of the conversation (if there is no talking it increases talking or if there is much talking, it eliminates talking) are good and critical questions for the team.

Basic Reflection Model
Outward Bound

Experience

Now What?
- What will you do differently next time?
- What will you do the same?

What?
- What happened?
- What did you see?
- What did you hear?
- What did you do?

So What?
- What worked?
- What did not work?
- How is this like what you tend to do in this situation?
- What assumptions did you make?
- What role did you play in the events?

Basic Reflection Model - outlines the sequencing of critical questions to be asked in the process of reflecting on experience.
- It is the practice of uncovering the unnoticed assumptions that drive our decisions.
- It seeks to create choice and challenge the validity of mental models
- It is an attempt to see things as they really are.
- It is a disciplined effort to learn from experience.

Collective Reflection Model

Shared Experience
Triggering Event/Behavior

Now What?
Align structures and processes with new learning that has occurred

What?
Map the group interaction using:
- Team Interaction Map
- Emotional Chains
- Team Contribution Map

So What?
- Of all the things that could have happened, why did this happen?
- What did that get the group?
- What values were dominant?
- What inconsistencies exist between stated values/assumptions and actual responses?

Critical Reflection

Tool: **Polarity Maps**

Purpose:

Many of the difficult issues in teams are really polarities that cannot be solved - only managed. Polarities are two seemingly opposing ideas that both are necessary over time for health and success. Often, those who resist change do so because they only see half of the issue. Polarity Maps are the work of Dr. Barry Johnson and is a tool for exploring both sides of the issue. (Polarity Management: Identifying and Managing Unsolvable Problems, Barry Johnson, HRD Press, 1992)

Instructions:
- Identify the polarity that you want to map.
- Each polarity has an upside and a downside. The upside is the positive things with that issue. The downside is what can happen when the focus is on that side of the polarity to the exclusion of the other side. It is also the characteristics that warn of imbalance. List the upside and the downside of each polarity.
- Ask the team to respond once they see the whole picture of the polarity. How are they doing with this? How does this help them think about the dynamics of their team? What does this teach them?

Facilitator Notes:
- As discussed in Chapter 2, some common polarities that teams need to think about are: the team vs. the individual, action vs. reflection, or stability vs. change.

The Stability vs. Change Polarity for Teams

Teams have two critical tasks that must both be accomplished in order for the team's success to be sustainable. First, they must have enough stability or defined boundaries to provide the structure and direction for them to chart their course. Yet, at the same time, the team must also continue to develop and enhance its ability to learn, change and adapt. The figure below outlines some of the upside and the downside of each end of this critical polarity. Both are necessary but neither are sufficient alone to make a sustainable team.

Effective Team

+
- Focused
- Clear roles
- Accountability
- Order
- Security

+
- Flexibility
- Adaptable
- Self-Renewing
- Innovative
- Continuous Learning

Stability | **Change**

- Rigid
- Static
- Limiting Initiative
- Reactive
- Irrelevant

- Chaotic
- Lack of focus
- Duplication of Effort
- Unguided

− **−**

Rigid and Dysfunctional

If you want to build teams to be successful at both ends of this polarity, you'll need to focus on two perspectives of teams. One perspective are things that can be engineered such as defining objectives, creating team norms, defining roles and aligning incentives. These are necessary actions that create stability for teams. Stabilizing factors provide the boundaries within which a team will work. Although necessary, they are not sufficient for team success. The other perspective to work on focuses on those things that must be grown in teams such as building trust, maturity, defining assumptions, including new members. These factors are considered dynamic because, unlike stabilizing factors, they cannot be addressed and left alone. The dynamic factors are things that must be monitored and developed all the time. They are the abilities that allow teams to continue to change and grow to address their ever changing environments.

Stabilizing Factors
- Direction
- Clear Purpose
- Common Objectives
- Defined Roles
- Team Norms

Dynamic Factors
- Managing Differences
- Adapting to Change
- Continuous Improvement
- Maintaining Trust
- Adopting New Members
- Challenging Assumptions

Critical Reflection

<u>Tool:</u> **Action Learning Process**

<u>Purpose:</u>

This is a process to teach teams that disciplines their interaction around the use of good questions to uncover assumptions and explore possible actions to resolve ongoing issues.

<u>Facilitator Notes:</u>
- It is assumed at this point that the facilitator has taken some time to define learning and the needed attitude that is being developed to the group.
- First, provide an overview of the process which includes the mindset, the process and the roles of an action learning team.
- Define the types of issues that are targeted by this process. This is an important and sometimes difficult hurdle for teams. The types of issues raised should be monitored closely in the beginning so that the team learns the process.
- Review the Dialogue Flow Diagram. This helps the team understand how the conversation should go. It is a good place to discuss a fatal flaw many teams have in this process which is to solve the issue too early without clearly defining the real issue.
- Discuss the issue template. Assign the team to identify and write out an issue they each may want to raise.
- Practice. Stop often, i.e. at the end of each issue, in the beginning to reinforce the discipline of the process and make needed adjustments. As the team learns the process, reflection on the process can move to the end of an entire action learning session instead of after each issue.

<u>Definitions:</u>
- **Set** – a group of learners who commit to coming together around many projects or a common project in order to reflect and learn from the planning and action that arises from their projects.
- **Project sponsor** – a person with organizational position, authority, resources and a stake in a project.

- **Learning Advisor** – a facilitator for the set that assists them in their group process and learning process.

The Elements of an Action Learning Process:

The Project or Issue
- The project must be a problem rather than a puzzle. A puzzle has a solution which has not been discovered by the learner yet. A problem is a situation to which there is no known solution.
- It should be real and challenging.
- It should have value for the organization.
- It should require not just data collection, planning and recommendations, but also action.

The Learner
- Non-defensive and growth oriented
- Open and curious
- Analytical and curious
- Creative and conceptual
- Innovative and willing to take risks
- Supportive and collaborative

The Set
- The set's purpose is to learn out of ignorance. That is members do not come to be an expert. They come to challenge one another's thinking about how they are solving the problems and what they are learning from their actions or attempts to solve problems.
- The set should be a small group 4-8 people.
- Best practice – meetings meet every 2 or 3 weeks at the beginning and move to a once a month.
- Time frame for set meetings – 4-5 persons 2-3 hours, 6-8 people a half day
- An up front commitment to a certain timeframe is advisable.

Dialogue Flow Diagram: The Path of Inquiry

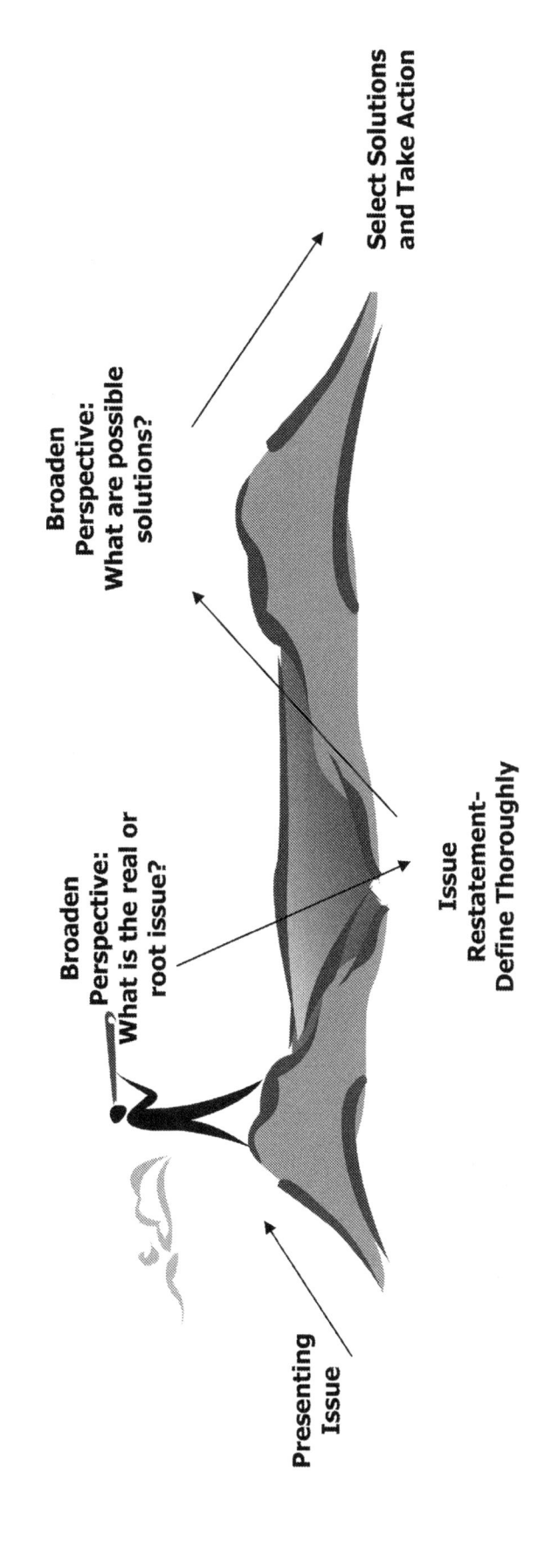

Presenting Issue

Broaden Perspective: What is the real or root issue?

Issue Restatement – Define Thoroughly

Broaden Perspective: What are possible solutions?

Select Solutions and Take Action

Teams for a New Generation 109

Action Learning Issue Template

Introduction:

As a participant in this course you are being asked to present issues to your action learning team as you apply the learning you are doing. The following template is meant to help you prepare your issue to share with the group. Please have the first two sections filled out when you come to your meetings. The last two sections will be answered in the group discussion.

Presenting Issue:
- What is the issue, action or circumstance that is being problematic?
- Why is this important to me?
- What assumptions am I making about this issue?

Describe Situation:
- Who is involved?
- What is the background of this team?
- When is this issue most obvious?
- What has been tried in the past?

Root Issues:

Actions to take:

Critical Reflection

<u>Tool:</u> **Team Interaction Map**

<u>Purpose:</u>
One of the reasons that teams repeat mistakes is that their process moves so fast they often only remember certain things that happened in an event. This combined with a tendency to look for single, linear explanations limits the team's ability to see the systemic connections. This tool allows a team to map a critical event, turning it from a movie to a snapshot. It is a method for diagramming the interaction of a group in order to assist in reflecting on that group's experience.

<u>Instructions:</u>
- In the boxes on the outer edges of the page, the facilitator should identify and record the most critical actions, decisions or events in the experience being mapped. It is important not to get too detailed because the map will get too complex. These critical actions should be in chronological order. (It helps if the facilitator or observers have recorded these as the experience happened to help keep things in order)
- In the white space to the center of the page, the facilitator/leader will note signs of importance. This is generally noting when anxiety goes up or down in the group. It is sometimes helpful to identify points of conflict or when new innovations or ideas are introduced to the group. These actions often come into play later than they appear in the sequence. In addition, the facilitator notes other ideas or thoughts that occur around this action that will help the team understand what was happening. Facilitators can also include important questions that should be asked about those circumstances.
- When complete, the group will have a snapshot of their experience. They can then begin to identify what assumptions the group was operating from. Also, it becomes possible to make connections between things that influenced one another but did not occur close in time. Ask reflection questions to help the team see these connections between actions and identify patterns of behavior as well as unexpected consequences.

Facilitator Notes:
- When mapping the experience, allow the team to build the chronological account with the facilitator or observers only filling in blank spots or correcting the order. Remember, you may discover that what the team thought was important differs from what the facilitator believes is important. Include all perspectives to get the best picture of the event.
- See Islands write-up in the Activities section.

Team Interaction Map Example

Objectives of the group:
1. Create an atmosphere of trust where team members ask for and give help to one another.
2. Develop open communication in order to avoid forbidden subjects.
3. Develop the ability of team members to speak up and take risks.
4. Continue with the performance measure process already underway.

Group:
15-18 Managers and supervisors

Activity:
Islands. The purpose of this activity was to create the conditions of multiple groups that were attempting to merge into one unified group.

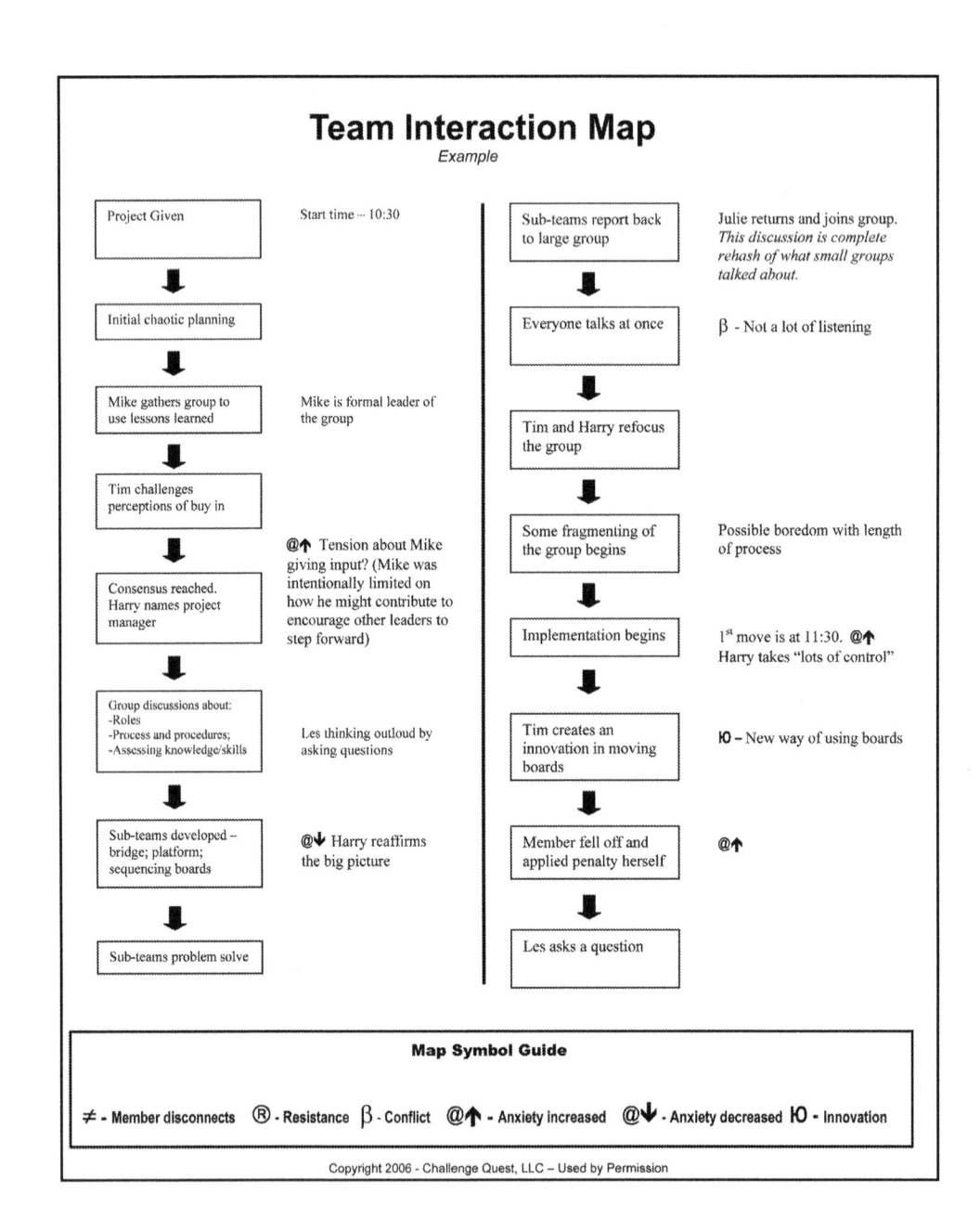

Team Interaction Map
Example

Project Given	Start time – 10:30
↓	
Initial chaotic planning	
↓	
Mike gathers group to use lessons learned	Mike is formal leader of the group
↓	
Tim challenges perceptions of buy in	
↓	@↑ Tension about Mike giving input? (Mike was intentionally limited on how he might contribute to encourage other leaders to step forward)
Consensus reached. Harry names project manager	
↓	
Group discussions about: -Roles -Process and procedures; -Assessing knowledge/skills	Les thinking outloud by asking questions
↓	
Sub-teams developed – bridge; platform; sequencing boards	@↓ Harry reaffirms the big picture
↓	
Sub-teams problem solve	

Sub-teams report back to large group	Julie returns and joins group. *This discussion is complete rehash of what small groups talked about.*
↓	
Everyone talks at once	β – Not a lot of listening
↓	
Tim and Harry refocus the group	
↓	
Some fragmenting of the group begins	Possible boredom with length of process
↓	
Implementation begins	1st move is at 11:30. @↑ Harry takes "lots of control"
↓	
Tim creates an innovation in moving boards	Ю – New way of using boards
↓	
Member fell off and applied penalty herself	@↑
↓	
Les asks a question	

Map Symbol Guide

≠ - Member disconnects   ® - Resistance   β - Conflict   @↑ - Anxiety increased   @↓ - Anxiety decreased   Ю - Innovation

Copyright 2006 - Challenge Quest, LLC – Used by Permission

Teams for a New Generation

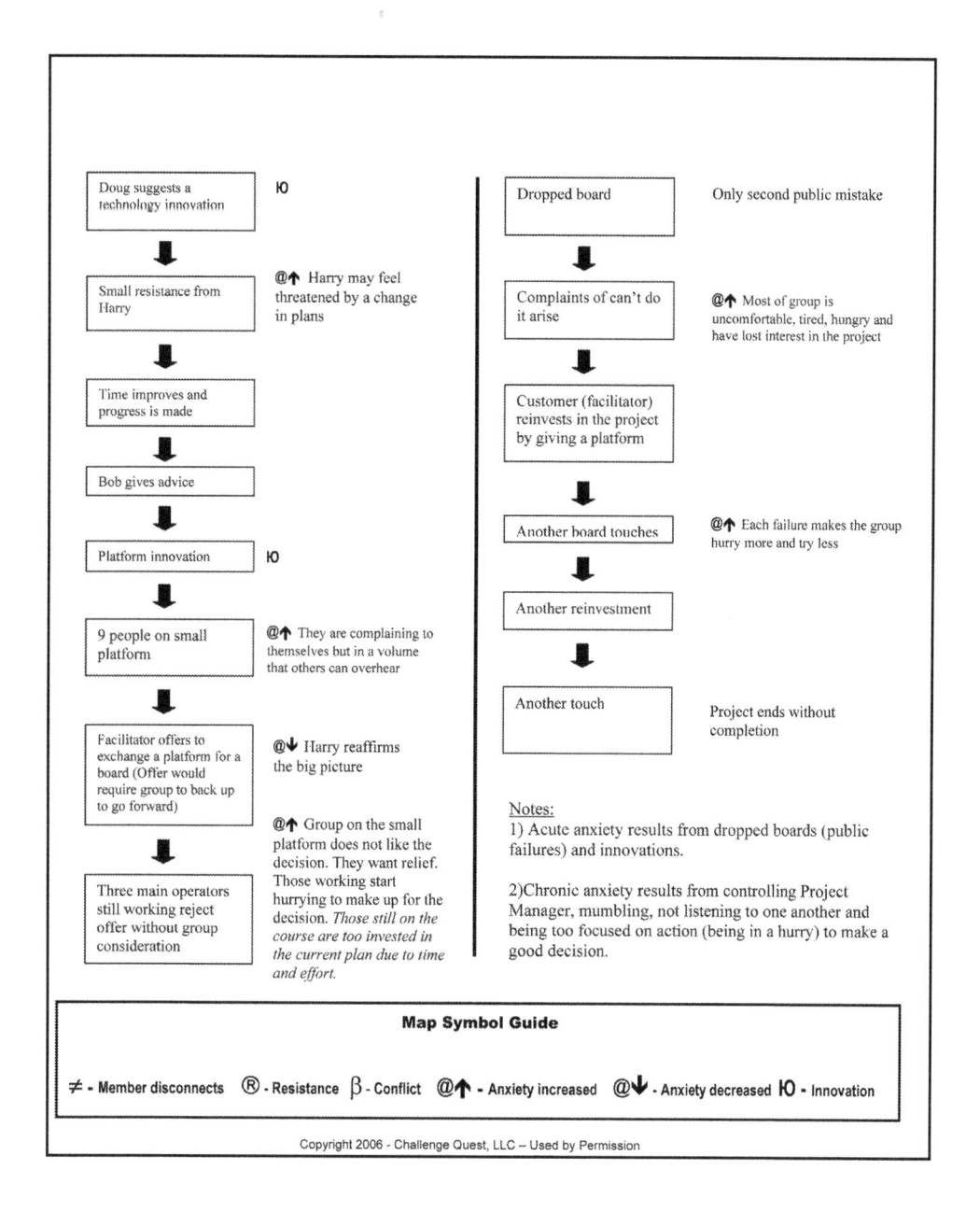

```
Doug suggests a            Ю
technology innovation
        ↓
                           @↑ Harry may feel
Small resistance from      threatened by a change
Harry                      in plans
        ↓
Time improves and
progress is made
        ↓
Bob gives advice
        ↓
Platform innovation        Ю
        ↓
                           @↑ They are complaining to
9 people on small          themselves but in a volume
platform                   that others can overhear
        ↓
Facilitator offers to
exchange a platform for a  @↓ Harry reaffirms
board (Offer would         the big picture
require group to back up
to go forward)
                           @↑ Group on the small
                           platform does not like the
        ↓                  decision. They want relief.
                           Those working start
Three main operators       hurrying to make up for the
still working reject       decision. *Those still on the
offer without group        course are too invested in
consideration              the current plan due to time
                           and effort.*
```

```
Dropped board              Only second public mistake
        ↓
                           @↑ Most of group is
Complaints of can't do     uncomfortable, tired, hungry and
it arise                   have lost interest in the project
        ↓
Customer (facilitator)
reinvests in the project
by giving a platform
        ↓
Another board touches      @↑ Each failure makes the group
                           hurry more and try less
        ↓
Another reinvestment
        ↓
Another touch              Project ends without
                           completion
```

Notes:
1) Acute anxiety results from dropped boards (public failures) and innovations.

2) Chronic anxiety results from controlling Project Manager, mumbling, not listening to one another and being too focused on action (being in a hurry) to make a good decision.

Map Symbol Guide

≠ - Member disconnects   ® - Resistance   β - Conflict   @↑ - Anxiety increased   @↓ - Anxiety decreased   Ю - Innovation

Copyright 2006 - Challenge Quest, LLC -- Used by Permission

Critical Thinking

<u>Tool</u>: **Team Contribution Map**

<u>Purpose:</u>
Teams who are in conflict or experience a chronic issue tend to believe that if only others would change then things would improve. A Team Contribution Map is a mapping technique to identify the mutual actions that create and sustain an unwanted conflict or way of working. It helps everyone see his or her contribution to the dynamics of the team which will help build systems thinking capability of the team.

<u>Instructions:</u>
Step 1 In the center box, write the chronic issue (i.e. an issue that refuses to be resolved) or conflict being considered by the team and how this issue manifests itself in the team's functioning.

Step 2 Draw a diagram and write in the names of the individuals on the team involved in the issue.

Step 3 <u>Option 1</u> – Have the team members fill in the outer boxes identifying what they believe each person contributes to keeping the issue or conflict in place. Then have each person read the contents of their boxes describing what each member did in their mind to contribute to this issue. Ask members to be sure to write in what others say about them in the box with their name in it. This should give each person a broader perspective of their impact on the issue.

<u>Option 2</u> – Move around the outer boxes and have the team brainstorm together out loud what they perceive as each person's contribution.

Step 4 Have each person reflect on their personal contributions by asking questions like:

- What do I hear this saying to me?
- What assumptions, values and beliefs do I have that drive this behavior?
- Of all the things I could do, why do I do this behavior?

Step 5 Create an individual development plan that would include at least these components:

- Do I want to change?
- If so, what do I need to learn?
- How will I learn what I need to learn?
- What do I need to unlearn?
- Who will support me in this effort?
- How will I know when I am being successful?

Facilitator Notes:
- This activity can be emotional so be sure to have the right environment set so that it does not become a giant finger pointing activity. The right environment would include an explicit agreement for people to understand their part and a willingness to change self in order to promote improvement.
- The outer boxes can also include departments or other organizations if that is appropriate to the situation.

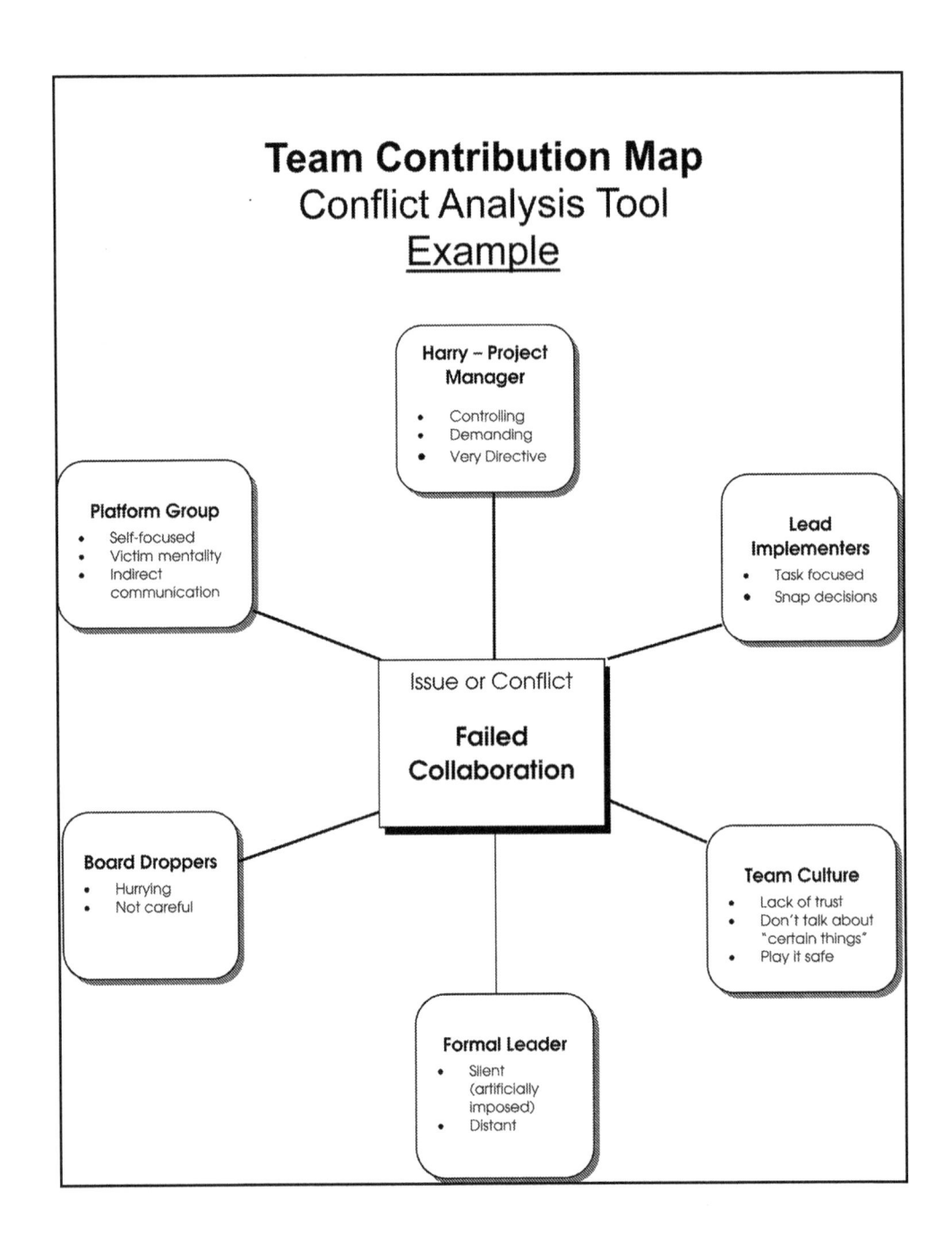

Team Contribution Map
Conflict Analysis Tool
<u>Example</u>

Harry – Project Manager
- Controlling
- Demanding
- Very Directive

Platform Group
- Self-focused
- Victim mentality
- Indirect communication

Lead Implementers
- Task focused
- Snap decisions

Board Droppers
- Hurrying
- Not careful

Team Culture
- Lack of trust
- Don't talk about "certain things"
- Play it safe

Formal Leader
- Silent (artificially imposed)
- Distant

Issue or Conflict
Failed Collaboration

Critical Reflection

Tool: **Structured Observation Worksheets**

Purpose:

There are always more things happening in a group situation than any one person can pay attention to. Consequently, it is important as a facilitator to be able to identify those things that are most important given the group's purpose. In an adult learning environment, it will be important to understand the behaviors that enhance collaboration (mutual discovery) and to contrast them with behaviors that inhibit or fragment the learning process. Here is a list of key actions that can be used to determine the potential for effective group learning process.

Facilitator Notes:
- Use the Structured Observation Worksheet to track participants actions in a given situation (meeting, activity, training, etc)
- After completion of the situation use the worksheet either individually or with the entire group to look at the behaviors of group members. Although the worksheet is just your opinion, you now have some data to work with and a place to begin the discussion for what is effective and what is not effective in the group's process.

Collaborative Actions – this is a category of behaviors that tend to promote learning, inquiry, reflection, the inclusion of others and the use of diversity to promote effective change. The behaviors are classified in 6 categories: proposing, clarifying questions, building, exploring, test understanding and bringing in.

Proposing – the observable behavior associated with proposing would include:

- Suggesting an alternative way of viewing an issue.
- Suggesting a new idea as a response to an issue or problem.
- Initiating any new topic of discussion.

Clarifying Questions – clarifying questions are questions aimed at getting a better understanding of the details of a situation. Questions are focused on concrete details not the underlying assumptions of an event or issue. These would include questions such as:

- Who?
- What?
- Where?
- When?

Building – these are behaviors that try to build on other ideas already suggested. It includes:

- Hitchhiking on the idea of another
- Integrating multiple ideas
- Connecting the current topic to other areas outside of the immediate context

Exploring – these are attempts to seek clarification and better understand the thinking (assumptions) behind an idea of another. These interactions might include questions like:

- How did you come to that conclusion?
- Can you say more about that idea?
- What experience have you had in this area?
- What do you mean?

Test Understanding – this is an attempt to check one's understanding of another person's perspective. It might include:

- Paraphrasing
- Repeating back to a person

Bring in – these are actions that are meant to include someone who has not been active in the interaction. It might include:

- Asking someone, "What do you think?"
- Suggesting a go around in order to hear from everyone.

<u>Fragmenting Actions</u> – this is a category of behavior that tends to divide or fragment the group. These tend to be defensive behaviors that work against change and learning, and support the status quo.

Defending/Attacking – these are automatic responses that suppress a different perspective, dismiss an idea without reflection or make overgeneralizations. This would include:

- Absolute statements – this will never work, he always does this
- Belittling with humor

Shutting out – these are behaviors that exclude people from conversations. This would include:

- Interrupting
- Ignoring
- Eye rolling
- Turning one's back on someone
- Walking away

Blaming – these are statements that shift responsibility to someone else. It could include:

- Blaming other people
- Blaming leadership
- Making excuses for one's own behavior due to environmental variables

Subgrouping – these are actions that communicate an informal, undeclared alliance of a part of the team to the exclusion of the rest of the team. It might include:

- Side conversations while someone is speaking
- Eye contact with an associated dismissing expression (eye rolling, grin, etc.)

Conflict Avoidance – these are actions taken to avoid confrontation or even opposing opinions. This might include:

- Quick explanations to divergent ideas
- Becoming silent rather than say something controversial
- Leaders telling others how it is
- Quickly changing the subject when the interaction becomes intense.

Structured Observation Worksheet

Behaviors	Leader	P1	P2	P3	P4	P5	P6	P7	P8
Collaborative									
Proposing									
Clarifying									
Building									
Exploring									
Test Understanding									
Bring in									
Fragmenting									
Defending – Attacking									
Shutting Out									
Blaming									
Subgrouping									
Conflict Avoidance									
Total Collaborative Actions									
Total Fragmenting Actions									

Group: **Date:** **Session time:**

Activities for Developing New Generation Teams

As useful as theory is to provide a language to discuss and describe physical actions, if it cannot be taught or passed on to others, its impact is minimal. We have focused our attention to this point on how facilitators can help teams develop Meta-skills to sustain their own success. Emotional Maturity and Critical Thinking are attitudes and skills that cannot be learned out of a book. They must be learned experientially. Too often we have talked to teams about what is required for them to be successful, only to have them agree but not be able to live it out. Intellectual understanding and agreement are not enough. Teams of a New Generation become so because they live into new ways of being. Consequently, the following section outlines exercises that we have found to be effective in helping to teach, practice and master the critical meta-skills of new generation teams. Not all of these activities are original to us; most are variations of activities we learned from other practitioners in the field. We appreciate their contributions.

ACTIVITIES

- Corporate Box
- Balster's Circle
- El Nino
- Balloon Bop
- Glass Ceiling
- Learning Dialogue Fishbowl
- Three Way Tug-O-War
- Yurt Rope
- Breathlessly Building
- Man in the Mirror
- Islands
- Ships Across the Sea
- Challenge Course Climbing Tower

Activity: Corporate Box

<u>Reference</u>: 1996 Activity Colloquium, Tulsa, Oklahoma

The 2008 Pfeiffer Annual: Training. Copyright © 2008 by John Wiley & Sons, Inc. Reprinted by permission of Pfeiffer, an Imprint of Wiley. www.pfeiffer.com

<u>Theme</u>: Awareness of Assumptions, Emotional Process

<u>Materials</u>: 80' rope; 8-10 squares; 2 hula hoops

<u>Setup</u>:

1. Create a rectangle on the floor with the dimensions approximately 15'x25'. For groups larger than 30 you can make this box larger. Place two hula hoops in the center of the rectangle. The rule of thumb is you want the box to be big enough so that participants cannot just step into the hula hoops in the middle.
2. Provide the group with 8-10 squares 12"x12". These can be made of carpet, foam shelving paper, or cloth. Be sure that the material of the squares does not cause a risk of slippage with the surface of the floor being used.

<u>Briefing</u>:

"In the fast paced corporate world that we find ourselves in, innovation, a willingness to take calculated risks and an openness to new ideas are valuable assets. A phrase that is often used to describe this kind of creative thinking is "out of the box" thinking. As we begin together today, our first project will be a living metaphor for what it means to move out of the box. Everyone needs to take a position on one of the four sides. As we begin to move out of our self-perceived limits, we do not move in just any direction. There is a purpose to our movement. For each of you this movement will be represented in your attempt to move across the square to the opposite side from where you are standing now. You will have all the resources necessary for you to make this move successfully and safely."

<u>Provide the following instructions</u>:

- To move, you must enter the box on the side you are now standing.

- If you do not utilize a resource or you misuse a resource, you will loose that resource.
- No one may touch the floor inside the rectangle. The consequence for this infraction is that everyone must begin again from their original position.
- A maximum of 2 feet can be on the squares at any time.
- If you choose to use the safe zones(hula hoops), a minimum of two feet must be inside the hoop or you lose them.

Paradigm Buster:
- After the group has successfully crossed the rectangle, you can offer the following challenge. The group must make the crossing in less than 15-60 seconds depending on the size of the group.
- A rule of thumb for the time frame for the paradigm buster is 25 people or less can do it in 15 seconds, 26-50 people can do it in 25 seconds, more than 50 people can do it in 30-45 seconds. Allow more time if there are physical limitations of the participants. The goal is to give them something that on the surface seems impossible. They will need to fail a time or two to bring out the power of the exercise.

Facilitator Points:
- It will be important to give the group all the information but do not over-engineer the activity. Most groups listen to about half of the instructions and have to learn through experience that not listening can be costly. This is a very important learning that should be discovered and not supplied by the facilitator.
- Many groups will initially work in isolation on their side of the box. Again, observe but do not over-control the activity. Let the group discover the limitations of not working together.
- A facilitator should expect a good deal of chaos at first. Everyone talks at once with many people sub-grouping. This is normal and should be tolerated for a time because again it is an important learning moment for the group.
- The facilitator should be anticipating the first time a participant lays down a square and looses contact with it. If the square is not being touched, it is not being utilized and should be taken away at once. Because they did not listen or check their understanding of what that

instruction means, this is often the group's first mistake. It is also the first time that they might stop and consider their process. It will be important to act quickly but not in a way that antagonizes the group. The facilitator is not out to get the resources. He/she is just enforcing the guidelines. Be prepared for shock, complaining and confusion from the group.

- When the paradigm buster is given the group will usually just try to do what they have already done again faster. It may take them a few iterations to realize that what helped them be successful before will not work now. They must challenge their assumptions because they have a working paradigm in place from their previous tries. This may be the most critical learning the group can take away given that facilitating learning is a different paradigm than training.

- The most effective solution we have seen is when the time starts, lay four resources in the four corners of the rectangle (see diagram below). Have one person keep a foot or hand on each resource and then have the rest of the group step into the box from the side there are now on and then out diagonally on the next side. They have now satisfied the guideline about entering the box. Now, people can walk around the outside of the box to get to their goal side. The Hula Hoops are just distractions and really don't need to be used. This type of solution fits and drives home the point (albeit tired and overused) of the introduction about people thinking 'outside of the box' literally. Another point can be about the Hula Hoops. Most groups struggle with trying to use the Hula Hoops and they really just slow the group down. But most groups will still try and use them because they are there.

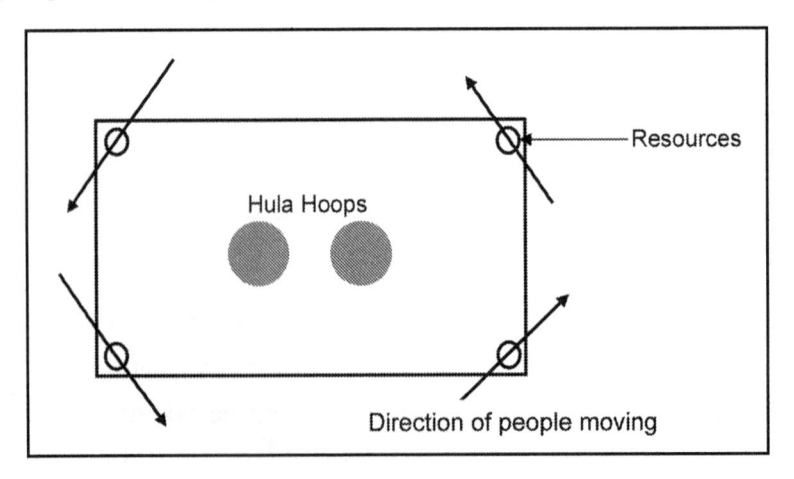

Activity: Balster's Circle

<u>Reference</u>: Steve Balster

<u>Theme</u>: Awareness of Assumptions, Influence of Anxiety

<u>Materials</u>: 45' rope; 4 carpet squares; 11 lifesize, puzzle pieces cut out of ¼" plywood. Use the template for one example of making the pieces to cut. One side will be painted red and the other side painted black. Make sure to take the middle piece out before you paint the other pieces. You will need to paint this piece opposite the colors of the other pieces. Example – if it fits together on the red side, paint that side black and then the other side red (Part of the paradigm buster is that the black middle piece fits with the other red pieces).

<u>Setup</u>:
1. Place a rope on the floor shaped like a circle that is about 10-15 feet in diameter. Place the large wooden puzzle pieces with red side up, unassembled inside the rope. Place 1-4 carpet squares around the outside of the rope circle. Note: This activity can also work well as a table top activity instead of on the floor.

<u>Briefing</u>:

"The very thing that makes teams so valuable is also a potential obstacle. What I am talking about is difference of perspective. The ability to clearly articulate what we see in a way that is helpful to others is an invaluable ability. In the following activity, this ability will be tested as your team tries to solve one of life's little puzzles."

<u>Provide the following instructions</u>:
- The group's job is to put the puzzle together. (You can place restrictions on how many pieces a person may touch if you want to involve more people. This also makes it more complex.)
- The only people who can touch the puzzle are those inside the circle.
- Once a person has touched a puzzle piece, they are the only person that can manipulate that piece.
- Those inside the circle must have their eyes shut at all times.

- You cannot move the rope.
- You cannot bring the puzzle pieces outside the circle.
- Those on the outside of the circle can only talk to those inside the rope if they are standing on a carpet square. If a group member is not standing on a carpet square, they can whisper to the people on the square but not loud enough for the person in the circle to hear.

Facilitator Points:
- To begin with, the team will have to challenge their assumptions about puzzles in at least two ways. First, for the pieces to fit correctly, the center piece must be turned upside down so that it is a different color than the rest of the puzzle. Second, there are straight-sided pieces that are usually associated with corners or edges that are interior pieces.
- Another place that teams usually form assumptions is around the use of the carpet squares for talking. Although the rope encircling the puzzle cannot be moved, nothing is said about the carpet squares. They can be moved and shared by more than one person at a time.
- This activity will also allow you to assess the self-regulation capability of team members. Notably, how anxious do members get watching someone else fumble with a project? Do they overreact, have a difficult time being quiet, or simply withdraw?

Template for Puzzle Pieces

```
┌─────────┬─────────┬─────────┐
│         │  RED    │         │
│  RED    │  RED    │  RED    │
│         │         │         │
├─────────┼─────────┼─────────┤
│  RED    │         │  RED    │
│         │  BLACK  │         │
│  RED    │         │         │
├─────────┼─────────┼─────────┤
│         │         │         │
│  RED    │  RED    │  RED    │
└─────────┴─────────┴─────────┘
         3-4 feet          (3-4 feet tall)
```

Paint the back side the opposite color

Activity: El Nino

Theme: Emotional Process

Materials: Tent pole (For a variation on this activity, use a hula hoop)

Setup:
1. Have the group divide themselves into two parallel lines facing each other.
2. Have them lift their arms and extend their index fingers, making a zipper out of the fingers. They should end up with a straight line of fingers in the middle of the two lines just above waist high.

Provide the following instructions:
The objective of the activity is to lay the tent pole that will be placed on their fingers on the ground. They have the following guidelines as they attempt the objective:

- They cannot just pull their fingers out and let the pole drop. It must be laid on the ground.
- They cannot place their fingers on top of the pole, pinch the pole or hook it with their fingers/thumbs. The pole must stay at rest on top of their fingers.
- Finally, their fingers cannot lose contact with the pole. If that happens, the group must start over.

Facilitator Points:
- This activity is an excellent example of emotional process and how a lack of awareness of the influence of anxiety makes even simple tasks very difficult.
- Most of the time, the team members, while trying to do the right thing, actually promote the opposite outcome than they are wanting, i.e. the pole goes up instead of down. This happens because members focus on others rather than themselves.
- One cause of this phenomena that helps explain emotional process is that members over-function. When a person over-functions he or she takes responsibility for things that are not their responsibility. In this activity, participants may start to monitor others, assign blame and try harder to control the situation to reduce the chaos that grows. What

they do not pay attention to is that while they are focused elsewhere, they push harder on the bottom of pole contributing to the worsening of the problem rather than a solution.

- Another teachable point is around reactivity. Teams struggle in this activity because they are unaware of the subtle reactions each person has to the rest of the team as everyone tries to maintain contact with the pole. Over time, all of these small reactions build into crisis as the task becomes impossible.
- Another key learning has to do with letting go and acceptance. In this activity if you try to prove that you are doing the right thing by touching the pole, you are actually making it worse. Only when the team stops, lets go of the need to direct others and allow the pole to touch them rather than they touching the pole, can progress be made.

Activity: Balloon Bop

Theme: Emotional Process, Personal Responsibility

Materials: 1 balloon for each person in group; 10-15 extra balloons; stopwatch

Setup:
1. Each person is asked to blow up a balloon and tie it. The facilitator will need an extra 10-15 balloons that are blown up and stored nearby.
2. The task is for the group to keep all the balloons in the air and in constant motion for a prescribed amount of time. Two minutes is a good goal.
3. While the team is focusing on keeping their balloons up, the facilitator continues to throw in additional balloons which also must be kept in the air. When a balloon (or for larger groups 3-4 balloons) touches the ground or comes to rest on something (a table, chair, a person's body) the time stops. The group is given a couple of minutes to see if they can come up with a strategy to improve performance.

Provide the group with the following instructions:
- Give everyone a single balloon.
- Have them blow up the balloon and tie it.
- Tell the group that the balloon they have represent their work or role in the team. They have a responsibility to do their job which means not allowing their balloon to touch the ground.
- Now there are also other tasks that are shared, require working across functions, unexpected requests or tasks that simply do not have any owner. These will be represented by the balloons that the facilitator will add to the mix. The team will also need to keep these balloons in the air as well.
- The goal is to keep the balloons in the air and moving by hitting them up with your hands for two minutes. If (whatever number of balloons touching the ground at the same time you want to set) touches occur, time will stop and we will start over. One thing to consider, the lower the number of balloons touching the ground, the more difficult the task gets. A typical number is 3 or 4 balloons touching the ground will bring time to a stop.

Facilitator Points:
- The key lesson out of this lesson is around the nature and impact of reactivity in the system. As new balloons are added and people start hitting the balloons harder, they create chaos which usually ends quickly in failure. Reactivity is the result of people over reacting to a situation. Remaining calm, staying in touch, and having an idea of how the team will divide up new work is the key.
- Another lesson that can be taught involves the stability vs. change paradox mentioned earlier in the book. Most teams believe that they are failing because they are not organized or structure correctly. So they work on trying to identify the "right" structure or arrangement. The truth is that if they do not understand the influence of the dynamic factors (reactivity, collaboration, and communication) no structure will work. Once they learn this, they will also discover that all sorts of forms of organization will work.
- Be ready for some frustration to grow. A good sequence may require the team go through 6 or 7 iterations before they figure out the cause and effect of their actions. Do not rescue the team if you want to experience the full power of this activity. The frustration accentuates the reactivity factor making the learning that much more powerful in the end.

Activity: Glass Ceiling

Theme: Emotional Process, Systems Thinking, Awareness of Assumptions

Materials: 1-5 balloons; stopwatch

Setup:

The object of this activity is for a group to keep a single balloon in the air and moving for two minutes. The guidelines are as follows:

1. The balloon must be kept in the air and moving. If it touches the ground or ceases to be moving, time stops and the team starts over.
2. The balloon cannot go higher than the top of the head of the tallest member of the group as they are standing on the ground. (The person cannot get on a chair to increase the height of the ceiling. If the balloon goes higher than the person's head, time stops and the group starts over.
3. Once a person has touched the balloon, everyone else must touch the balloon before that person can touch it again. If the balloon is touched out of sequence, time stops and the group starts over.
4. *Optional* – if you want to increase the difficulty of the activity, restrict the group from using their hands (defined as anything below their wrists).

Provide the group with the following instructions:
- Your task is to keep this balloon in the air and moving for 2 minutes.
- The balloon cannot be wedged, stuck with static electricity on the wall or ceiling, nor can it be held. If it is time will stop and you will start over.
- The balloon cannot touch the ground or come to rest on any table, chair, etc. or time will stop and you will start over.
- The balloon cannot go higher than the height of the tallest member of the group as they are standing on the ground. This means that you cannot stand on anything to increase the height limit. If the balloon goes too high, time will stop and you will start over.
- Once you have touched the balloon, everyone else must touch it before you touch it again. If the balloon is touched out of sequence, time will stop and you will start over.

Facilitator Points:
- There are several lessons that can come out of this activity. One is that assumptions we make around time. Groups tend to get in a hurry and try to move the balloon as quickly as they can around the circle (the most common formation). This is the opposite of what they need. The slower the balloon goes the less work they have to do and the fewer opportunities occur for mistakes. Yet, when time is involved, we tend to think faster.
- Again, if people over react by hitting the balloon hard, they disrupt the flow and cause the entire system to fail.
- It is a good activity to teach systems thinking with. Often the person who makes the move that stops the time gets blamed for the act, but it may have started one or two people prior to the person where the failure actually occurs. If a person makes a bad pass and that is compounded by another bad pass, the failure is the result of several contributing factors not just the person who finally stops the clock.

Activity: Learning Dialogue Fishbowl

Theme: Managing Differences, Emotional Process, Awareness of Assumptions

Materials: Most Dangerous Job ranking sheets; MDJ expert answer sheet; pens; paper

Setup:
1. Divide the group in half. Half of the group will form the discussion group that will take part in the activity. Their objective is to have as many right answers as they can when the expert answers are provided from the activity. In the end, they will be evaluated by how right their answers are and nothing else.
2. The other half of the group forms a fishbowl. Their objective is to observe the conversation the other half of the group is having around the activity. The observers are to make notes on what they see. They are instructed to watch specifically for those behaviors that either invites more conversation and thus more learning or those behaviors that push people away from the conversation and thus inhibits learning.
3. After the activity, the facilitator will lead a debriefing session that will explore the conversation. The group doing the activity should talk about what they experienced first. The observers then share what they saw. The facilitator fills in any gaps at the end.

Briefing:
"Ask most people why teams are formed and at least one answer almost always shows up -- diversity. In theory many confess that a group of people are nearly always smarter than the individual. In practice, the diversity that promised so much strength is in the end what limits the team's effectiveness. The reason being, allowing the difference of perspective, opinion and experience to challenge a person's or group's current thinking is not an easy task. Even with groups that are good natured, familiar and willing to learn, managing difference and using that difference to make the group smarter takes awareness, courage and a good deal of purposefulness. The following activity is designed to surface the dynamics of a group's tendency to deal with difference. In the end, the group will be able to determine if they are talking to confirm or are they talking to learn."

Provide the group with the following instructions:
- Pass out the Most Dangerous Jobs ranking sheets to the people in the discussion group.
- Have the team members quietly (without talking) rank the items on the list from most dangerous to least dangerous. This should take no more than 5 minutes.
- After the five minutes, give the discussion group time to talk about their answers and ask questions of each other. If anyone wants to change their answers they are welcome to. This takes about 15-20 minutes.
- After the discussion time, debrief the activity with the sequence mentioned above in the setup

Facilitator Points:
- The primary focus for the facilitator in this exercise is what does the group do with difference of opinion? You may notice one of two things.
- Someone will have very different answers from the rest of the group. What does the group do with that difference?
- Often they will use humor to brush aside the different opinion and will move quickly back to another line of thought.
- The other thing that may happen is the group will try to convince the one with a different perspective to change their mind.
- Everyone will agree. In this case, the members will confirm each others answers. What will be noticeably absent is any attempt to surface a different perspective, answer or frame of reference.
- In both of these cases, the group is talking to confirm what they already know rather than talking to learn from each other.
- The facilitator may also see the group quickly move to trying to reach or force consensus even though consensus was never a part of their instructions. This may be a mechanism to reduce their anxiety about the possibility of being wrong.
- This exercise also provides an excellent opportunity to highlight what teamwork means in a knowledge age. Teamwork is more often a mindset that allows others to influence a person and generally takes place in the pursuit of a common end. The quote below really does a good job of

highlighting the difference between cooperation (traditional notions of teamwork) and collaboration (teamwork in the knowledge age).

From the Program on Social and Organizational Learning at George Mason University:

"When people engage with each other in jointly striving toward a shared intention, the seeds of collaboration have been planted. Yet, collaboration entails far more. As they build relationships that are well grounded in honesty and trust, as they respect their varied talents and experiences, as they value and seek each other's contributions, and as they gently but firmly accept personal responsibility and hold each other accountable, collaborative work begins.

Collaboration requires far more than cooperation--where each person remains autonomous and toleration may best describe their interaction, meaning that the individuals are not fundamentally changed by their relationship. In collaborative relationships, there is a mutuality of influence and learning that enables each person to grow beyond what would have been possible for either individual alone."

Most Dangerous Job Ranking Sheet

	1 Your Individual Ranking	2 The Team's Ranking	3 Expert's Ranking
1. Driver/Sales Workers and Truck Drivers			
2. Farmers and Ranchers			
3. Fishers and Fishing Workers			
4. Miscellaneous Agricultural Workers			
5. Electrical Power Line Installers/ Repairers			
6. Refuse and Recyclable Material Collectors			
7. Logging Workers			
8. Aircraft Pilots			
9. Structural Iron and Steel Workers			
10. Construction Laborers			

Most Dangerous Job Expert Answer Sheet

Job	Fatality Rate
1. Fishers and fishing workers	118.4
2. Logging workers	92.9
3. Aircraft pilots	66.9
4. Structural iron and steel workers	55.6
5. Refuse and recyclable material collectors	43.8
6. Farmers and ranchers	41.1
7. Electrical power line installers/repairers	32.7
8. Driver/sales workers and truck drivers	29.1
9. Miscellaneous agricultural workers	23.2
10. Construction laborers	22.7

Source: *U.S. Bureau of Labor Statistics, 2005, Based on fatality rate per 100,000*

Activity: Three Way Tug-o-War

<u>Theme</u>: Systems Thinking, Conflict Resolution, Emotional Process

<u>Materials</u>: 1 carabiner; 3 ropes

<u>Setup</u>:
1. Tie a loop on the end of two ropes and connect them with a carabiner in the middle.
2. Lay out the two ropes in a straight line, much like you would for a standard tug of war contest.
3. Ask the group to split in half and pick up their end of the rope. (I do not give a lot of information in the first 30 seconds they are holding the rope. Most of the time the groups will start tugging the rope on their own.)
4. Make sure the group has tension on the rope. This is the first teaching point.
5. Ask the group to describe various strategies for winning a tug-o-war.
6. Ask the group which one of the strategies is their personal favorite.
7. Describe a very common way for people to keep conflicts alive without really dealing with the situation – Triangles.
8. Attach a third rope to the center carabiner, which is to be held by the facilitator.
9. Using the third rope, the facilitator pulls in different directions to highlight the different ways triangles work.
10. Finally, have the group think of a way that allows everyone to "win" but uses the tension in the rope. You may have to talk about what "winning" feels like to stimulate thinking. Remember do not let the group off with just taking turns with one side having fun while the other side "works". Both sides are to experience "winning" at the same time. Some common outcomes are: create a circle and balance the team (much like a yurt rope), creating a centrifuge with teams spinning in a circle, balancing in a straight line while letting the very end persons layout towards the ground.

Facilitator Points:
- Too many people believe tension in a relationship means there is something wrong. However, tension can be a creative force depending on how we respond to it.
- The most common ways of winning a tug-o-war are also the most common ways of dealing with conflict:
  - Dig in and wait the other side out
  - Deception and misdirection
  - Brute force, over powering the other side
  - Walking away and not playing at all
- Many times conflict is prolonged because we tend to see conflict in terms of a linear cause, i.e., one side is wrong and is causing the conflict. A systemic way of thinking about conflict is to see it in terms of the relationship. Conflict is an indication that the interactions of the relationship between two or more people are not working. All sides contribute something. If the parties can understand this, they can work together to attack the common enemy – dysfunctional interactions— rather than fighting each other.
- A very common way for conflict to be dealt with is the creation of Triangles. Triangles are created when one of the parties in tension brings something or someone else in the situation to ease the immediate anxiety of the conflict. This can look like:
- Getting a third party to side with them against the other member of the conflict
- Focusing on someone else as the scapegoat
- Creating a temporary alliance against the third party or issue thus creating false cohesion.
- When a Triangle exists, the parties that are truly responsible for the tension push that responsibility to someone else. The third party in a triangle often bears the anxiety of the two who will not deal with their issues.
- The key to avoiding Triangles is to consistently work to push responsibility to its rightful owner. Do not fall into blaming which is a telltale sign of Triangles.

Activity: Yurt Rope

<u>Theme</u>: Systems Thinking, Personal Responsibility, Emotional Process

<u>Materials</u>: 30' rope

<u>Setup</u>:
1. Have each participant take a hold of the rope with both hands and back up to extend the loop.
2. Then have each person raise their hands above their heads and step into circle. This will allow them to place the rope behind them.
3. Participants should then place the rope in a comfortable place somewhere near the middle of their low back.
4. Have everyone lean back on the rope until everyone is balanced on the rope.
5. Now you can begin to illustrate the nature of systems.

<u>Facilitator Points</u>:
1. When balanced, you have created a system – a set of interdependent, mutually influencing relationships.
2. Also, make the point that everyone has influence in the system. Each contributes in some way to the current state of the system.
3. The next point to make is that in systems, small changes can have large outcomes. As the facilitator, begin to slowly shift your weight against the rope so that others begin to adjust as a result.
4. In addition to small changes having big results, changes can be initiated from all parts of the system.
5. The final point is that the real power in a system is to focus on changing yourself rather than changing others.
6. To demonstrate this point, ask the group to make you stand up straight. Generally, they will all start pulling hard on the rope. The facilitator should resist. The more they pull, the greater the resistance. The answer is that if they will let go, the facilitator will have to stand up or fall down. The moral is if we change ourselves, others will also change, but as long as we try to change others, we cannot learn from each other. We will only resist each other.

Activity: Breathlessly Building (with a twist)

<u>Reference</u>: Adapted from 1993 Oklahoma State University Camp Redlands Play Day

<u>Theme</u>: Systems Thinking; Difference between Competition and Collaboration

<u>Materials</u>: 1 60' rope (designates the work area); 5 Hula-Hoops; 50-60 Wooden or Styrofoam blocks (2' X 4' X 10"); 4 Entrance markers (anything that signifies an entrance to the work area such as cones, masking tape, etc.)

<u>Setup</u>:

With the perimeter rope, lay out a large circle with enough room for 5 hula-hoops and space in between areas (see diagram). Place one hoop in the very center of the work area. This is where all the building resources go. Make sure they all fit inside the hoop! Set up the remaining four hoops as shown in the diagram.

Divide the group into 4 equal sized groups. Each group or 'department' has their own respective hoop and entrance to the work area.

<u>Briefing</u>:

Explain that the goal is for each group to build the tallest, freestanding structure, in their hoop using only the resources provided from the resource hoop. They have 10 minutes to complete this objective.

<u>Provide the group with the following instructions</u>:
- The only resources that are available are those in the resource hoop.
- You may not steal resources from other hoops.
- Only one person from each group may be inside the work area at a time.
- You must hold your breath the entire time you are in the work area. When your breath runs out, your turn is over.
- Everyone in the group must have a turn in the work area before the same order is repeated.

Facilitator Points:
- After the ten minutes has passed, stop all work. Explain that because of changes within the organization, job responsibilities have changed and as a result, each group rotates clockwise to the next groups' hoop, leaving their work behind. Thus, Group 1 now works at Group 2's hoop, 2 at 3's, 3 at 4's, and 4 at 1's (groups may not take resources with them when the move). Inform everyone they now have 10 more minutes to complete the objective.
- You may rotate up to 4 times depending on time, but allow yourself at least 2 rotations (30 total minutes of construction time).
- Another way the group might 'solve' the problem is to have all 4 groups decide to build a structure in one hoop. They decide that this is everyone's hoop. Groups work together in completing the objective, which results in one structure with all of the resources instead of four structures with some of the resources. If this happens, you can highlight the differences between competition and collaboration.
- Debrief the activity using processing questions.

Breathlessly Building (with a Twist) Layout

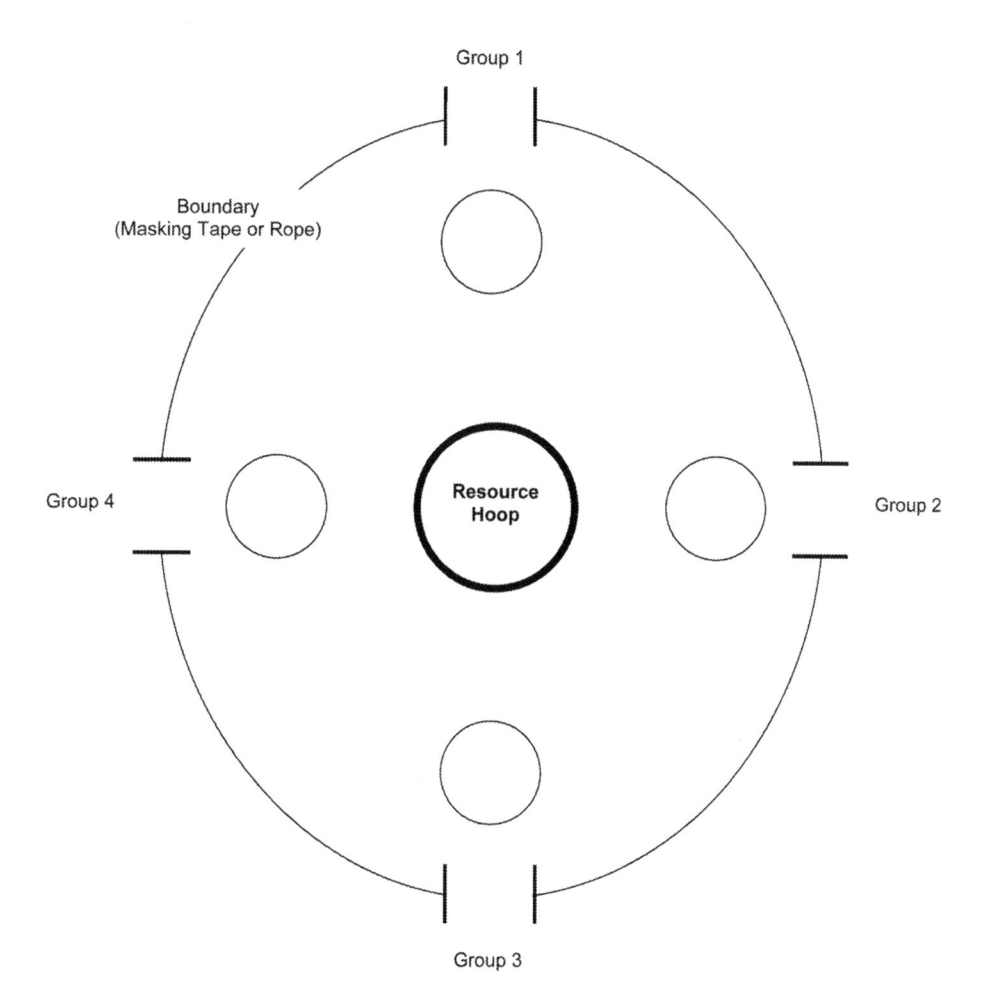

- Group 1 (top)
- Group 2 (right)
- Group 3 (bottom)
- Group 4 (left)
- Boundary (Masking Tape or Rope)
- Resource Hoop (center)

Activity: Man in the Mirror

<u>Reference</u>: Challenge Quest, LLC

<u>Theme</u>: Critical Thinking

<u>Materials</u>: Mirror for each person

<u>Briefing</u>:

"You have a mirror. You are being asked to look into the mirror and reflect on what you see as you look into your own eyes. Please, look beyond the obvious. It is an assumption that you will see physical details about your appearance. The question for you to wrestle with is when you look into your heart, mind and soul, what do you see? The following set of questions is a guide that demonstrates a model for reflection. Please do not limit yourself to these questions. They are only a place to start."

What? What do you see?

So What? Thinking about what you have listed, what do you think these observations mean? Why are these observations important to you?

Now What? You have now increased your awareness about yourself. How will that influence you?

<u>Facilitator Points</u>:
- This exercise can lead to a number of insights. The first place to look is at what the participants actually say they see. This is what they are paying attention to. Is it balanced? By that do they seem to see both positive and negative aspects of themselves? Is it proportional, i.e. do their observations seem too extreme?
- Secondly, we like to discuss how they experienced the process of introspection. What was it like for them? Most people claim they are very uncomfortable with introspection. Self-awareness is the corner stone of the type of teams that we have been discussing. This is a foundational skill. We like to explore what made them so uncomfortable. This can provide some suggestions about their threshold of emotional discomfort and possible points of reactivity for that person.

Activity: Islands

Reference: Adapted by Challenge Quest, LLC

Theme: Systems thinking and emotional process

Materials: 5 platforms 30"x 30", 1 – 6' board (2x8" preferred), 2 – 4' boards, 1 – 3' board

Setup:
- Set the platforms up in a diamond formation with one platform in the center of the diamond.
- Place boards on three of the outer platforms.
- The platforms should be spaced so that no individual board can reach between any two platforms alone.

Provide the group with the following instructions:
- Split your group into three fairly even sub groups and go stand by one of the three platforms with boards laying on them.
- The goal is to move your groups from your starting platform to the platform at the far tip of the diamond formation. For the group to successfully complete the project you must end up with everyone "on the same page" and off the ground at the final platform.

Some guidelines include:
- You cannot jump. This means that you must always have one foot in contact with wood.
- You cannot touch the ground. If you do, you go back to your original platform and start again.
- The boards cannot touch the ground. If they do, they will go away.

Safety concerns:
- Watch for splinters. Be careful of running your hand up and down the boards.
- Watch when you are moving boards around. Be careful not to hit people around you with a board.
- Be careful not to strain you back when lifting and extending boards. Get help if you need extra strength to move a board.

- Watch when you shift weight on boards that are extended off the sides of a platform. You can dump people quickly if they are not aware.
- Watch for boards spinning out from under you when you take a big step.

Facilitator Points:
- The first thing that often with teams that get these instructions is that they get very anxious about having to end with everyone on the final platform (on the same page) at the same time. They cannot conceive how this might be possible. For teams that must be certain, they may have a tough time even getting started because they cannot know for sure what the end result will look like.
- Second, pay attention to what is said and done by those who reach the end platform first. People who reach this point often check out, assuming that they are done. They also grow increasingly more anxious because they are forced to stand very close to people on a small platform for a long time. Their anxiety can show up through indirect comments that may sound like complaining or some urgent call for this activity to end. This can have a rippling effect on the emotional process of the team (see the team interaction map on the next page). As their anxiety increases and is made known to the team, the team may try to hurry causing them to make mistakes. Or, the team may get distracted in relieving the discomfort of the few and leave a process that is working to make those at the end comfortable. This can lead to a loss of focus, strategy and multiple mistakes.
- Another place to watch is decision making. How are decisions made and resources allocated? Frequently decisions are made by the loudest. As isolated members make decisions that impact the rest of the team, the team's anxiety will increase. But this issue is rarely addressed directly. Competing, unspoken agendas of power can emerge. This is a systems process requiring systems thinking to see it. There are multiple contributing factors that lead to the decision making process. The team must see all of them to really understand how they arrived at this kind of dynamic.
- The solution to then end comes by the facilitator negotiating with team for more or redistributed resources. Typically, when a team clears one of the outer platforms of all people, the facilitator can offer them

additional boards or to move the empty platform to the end. The team should choose the resource they want, but the facilitator should choose where the resources are moved, especially the platforms. You do not want to place a new platform in a position that allows any of the boards to span between platforms alone.

Layout:

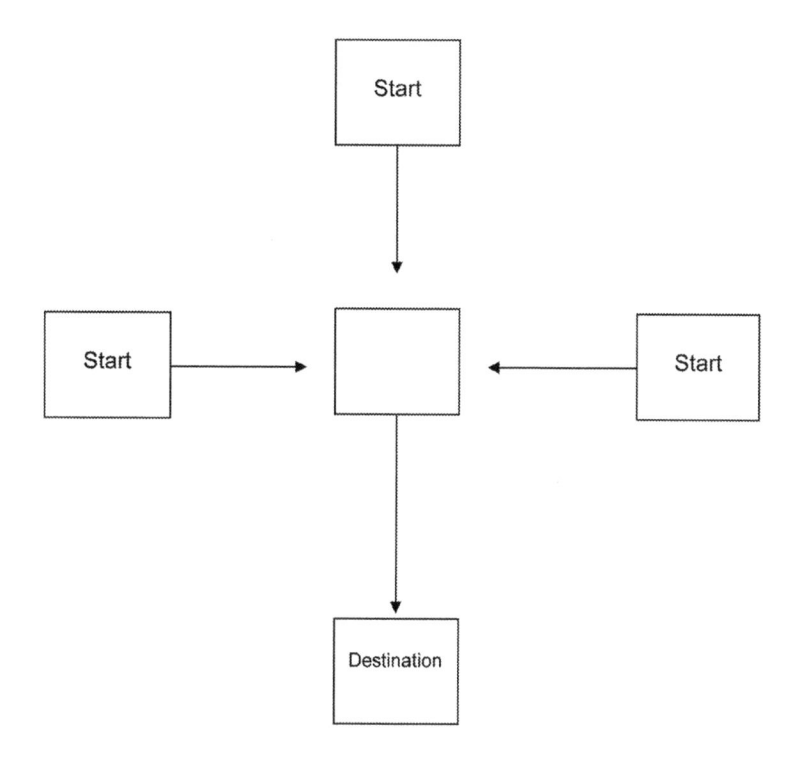

```
                    ┌─────────┐
                    │  Start  │
                    └────┬────┘
                         │
                         ▼
┌─────────┐         ┌─────────┐         ┌─────────┐
│  Start  │────────▶│         │◀────────│  Start  │
└─────────┘         └────┬────┘         └─────────┘
                         │
                         ▼
                    ┌─────────────┐
                    │ Destination │
                    └─────────────┘
```

See Team Interaction Map of this activity in the Tools section

Activity: Ships Across the Sea

Theme: Emotional Maturity

Materials: One blindfold

Setup:
One person is blindfolded and will attempt to cross a determined distance (20-40 feet) without hitting any obstacles. The rest of the group arrange themselves as obstacles within the space. The obstacles can be in any arrangement, however, they cannot move once the ship (the blindfolded person) has begun to cross. The ship may ask for help from the obstacles (also known as mines) at any time. The mines can only give directions if they are asked and only the mines closest to the ship may speak.

Briefing:
"Giving and receiving feedback is a two-way street. It is often something that does not go well because either opinions are offered when they are not wanted or the person receiving the help is not open to being helped. This activity will provide a place to practice giving and receiving help." (Then provide the instructions above).

Facilitator Points:
One of the hardest things for an emotionally immature person to do is to stand back and let other people struggle or even just figure things out on their own. In this activity, those who struggle with this will struggle with not helping and waiting to be asked to help. The person who has a low tolerance for emotional discomfort will begin to take over (or over-function) for others.

Possible Debriefing Questions:
- How well did you follow the directions given to you?
- What was most difficult about the activity?
- How did it feel to be the ship? Were you empowered or controlled?
- As you think about this activity, what has stuck out in your mind the most?

- Why do you think it is so difficult to use builders rather than barriers?
- What are some specific examples of builders or barriers that occur in your everyday situation?
- How will you use this information?

Activity: Challenge Course Climbing Tower

Theme: Emotional Awareness, Emotional Process, Courage

Emotional Awareness Definition:
- Emotional awareness involves the ability to monitor and manage the emotional atmosphere in the team without becoming reactive to one another.
- It recognizes the influence emotions have on behavior and seeks to make actions more intentional and less automatic.

Courage Definition:
- It is the ability to be comfortable enough with discomfort to allow learning to take place.
- It is the choice to do the right thing in the face of difficulty.

Materials: Climbing Wall on Challenge Course

Briefing:
"Learning and changing can cause us to feel some anxiety due to the fact that we are uncertain as to how things will come out and we may need to let go of some control while we learn from and with others. In addition to general uncertainty of learning something new, when the pressure is on we experience even more anxiety. When this occurs we tend to have some automatic responses that make us feel better. Learning to pay attention to our inner processes in the "heat of the moment" and having the courage to make the right choice will make the difference between real success and mediocrity. What we want is for you to enter a stressful situation (climbing the tower) and do the following:

1. Pay attention to your inner processes (especially feelings) so we can explore them later.
2. Ask for your fellow learners to help you figure things out when you need it.
3. Help those who are climbing find their options."

Debrief:
- Use Emotional Chains to explore their actions.
- Reflect on how they worked and helped each other during the climb.

- *Why do you think emotional awareness and courage are important to being a leader?*

Learning Points:
1. This is critical to a leader. Leader's who are not aware of or do not manage their own fear end up making others subject to the leader's fears.
2. For the leader who wants to be capable of doing a good job in this area consistently, he/she must come to understand where their source of value comes from. A leader who does not know who he/she is and who does not come to accept their own innate value, will find themselves doing many ineffective things to prove themselves.
3. What a facilitator should watch for is the tone, direction and content of the encouragement that the members on the ground are providing the climber, especially once the climber gets stuck. Often team members on the ground start yelling instructions, but they are instructions that take over for the climber. They do not provide choices to the climber they direct the climber and start "micro-managing" the climb. One meaning for this can be that the team members on the ground are so uncomfortable with the climber who is struggling that they take an easy way out for the team members on the ground. By taking control, the team members alleviate their own anxiety. Their actions are driven by their own discomfort more so than the needs of the climber.

Notes

Chapter 1

1. H. Nouwen, *Reaching out* (New York: Image, 1975).

Chapter 2

1. M. J. Wheatley & M. Kellnor-Rogers, *Bringing Life to Organizational Change*, Journal of Strategic Performance Measurement, April/May pp. 5-13, 1998.

2. B. Johnson, *Polarity Management: Identifying and Managing Unsolvable Problems* (Amherst, MA: HRD Press, 1992).

Chapter 3

1. See, for example, P. Senge, *The Fifth Discipline* (New York: Currency Doubleday, 1990); C. Argyris, *Overcoming Organizational Defenses: Facilitating Organizational Learning* (Needham Heights, MA: Allyn and Bacon, 1990); J. Mezirow, *Transformative Dimensions of Adult Learning* (San Francisco: Jossey-Bass, 1991); D. Schon, *The Reflective Practitioner* (New York: Basic Books, 1990).

2. See, for example, F. Pearls, *Gestalt Therapy Verbatim* (Moab, Utah: Real People Press, 1969); D. Bohm, *On Dialogue* (London: Routledge, 1996); M. Bowen, *Family Therapy in Clinical Practice* (New York: Jason Aronson, Inc, 1978); C. Argyris, *Overcoming Organizational Defenses: Facilitating Organizational Learning*.

3. W. N. Isaacs, *Taking Flight: Dialogue, Collective Thinking and Organizational Learning*. Organizational Dynamics, (Vol. 22, 24-40, 1993, p. 98).

Chapter 4

1. G. Robinson, & M. Rose, *A Leadership Paradox: Influencing Others by Defining Yourself – Revised Edition* (Indiana: AuthorHouse, 2006).

2. M. S. Peck, *The Different Drum* (New York: Touchstone, 1987).

3. B. Tuckman, *Developmental Sequence in Small Groups*. Psychological Bulletin (Vol. 63. No. 6. 1965, pp. 384-399).

4. Hesselbein, Frances & Goldsmith, Marshall editors. *Leaders of the Future 2* (San Francisco: Jossey-Bass, 2006).

Chapter 5

1. A. Amussen, *Workplace stressors in corporate systems: a theoretical model*. Progress: Family Systems Research and Therapy (Volume 5, Encino, CA: Phillips Graduate Institute, 1996, pp. 111-126).

2. P. Steinke, *How Your Church Family Works* (New York: Alban Institute, 1993).

3. M. S. Peck, *The Different Drum, p. 91*.

4. J. J. Voyer, J. M. Gould, D. N. Ford, *Systematic creation of organizational anxiety*, The Journal of Applied Behavioral Psychology (Nov-December, 1997, pp.471-89).

5. S. M. Abdullah, *Creating a World that Works for All* (San Francisco: Berrett-Koehler, 1999).

Chapter 6

1. E. Schein, *Process Consultation: Its Role in Organization Development* (Reading, MA: Addison Wesley Publishing Company, 1969).

2. P. Kline & Saunders, B, *Ten Steps to a Learning Organization* (Arlington, VA: Great Ocean Publishers, Inc, 1993, p.207).

3. Ibid, p. 204.

4. C. Argyris, *Overcoming Organizational Defenses: Facilitating Organizational Learning*; E. Friedman, *Generation to Generation* (New York: Guliford Press, 1986).

5. P. Senge, *The Fifth Discipline*.

6. J. Gleick, *CHAOS: Making a New Science* (New York: Penguin Books, 1987).

Chapter 7

1. G. Robinson, Unpublished personal journal, 1993.

2. T. Grant, *The Silence of Unknowing* (Liguori, MO: Triumph Books, 1995, p.91).

Chapter 8

1. D. Bohm, *On Dialogue*; L. Ellinor & G. Gerard, *Dialogue* (New York: John Wiley & Sons, 1998); W. N. Isaacs, *Taking Flight: Dialogue, Collective Thinking and Organizational Learning*.

2. M. S. Peck, *The Different Drum*.

3. L. Ellinor & G. Gerard, *Dialogue*.

4. Ibid.

5. T.S. Geisel & T.S. Geisel, *Green Eggs and Ham* (New York: Random House, 1960).

6. L. Ellinor & G. Gerard, *Dialogue*.

7. Ibid.

8. P. Senge, A. Kleiner, C. Roberts, R. Ross, & B. Smith, *The Fifth Discipline Fieldbook* (New York: Currency Doubleday, 1994).

Bibliography

Abdullah, S. M. Creating a World that Works for All. San Francisco: Berrett-Koehler, 1999.

Albom, M. Tuesdays with Morrie. New York: Doubleday, 1997.

Amussen, A. *Workplace Stressors in Corporate Systems: A Theoretical Model.* Progress: Family Systems Research and Therapy, Volume 5 (pp111-126). Encino, CA: Phillips Graduate Institute, 1996.

Argyris, C. Overcoming Organizational Defenses: Facilitating Organizational Learning. Needham Heights, MA: Allyn and Bacon, 1990.

Bardill, D. The relational systems model for family therapy: living in the four realities. Binghamton, NT: The Haworth Press, 1997.

Bohm, D. On Dialogue. London: Routledge, 1996.

Bolman, L. & Deal, T. Leading with Soul. San Francisco: Jossey-Bass Publishers, 1995.

Bowen, M. Family Therapy in Clinical Practice. New York: Jason Aronson, Inc, 1978.

Covey, S. The Seven Habits of Highly Effective People. New York: Fireside, 1989.

Ellinor, L., & Gerard, G. Dialogue. New York: John Wiley & Sons, 1998.

Fitzgerald, L. A. *Living on the edge.* <http://www.ormind.com/chaos/living.html> (December 22, 1997).

Friedman, E. *Reinventing Leadership.* (video and viewer guide). New York: Guliford Press, 1996.

Friedman, E. Handbook of Family Therapy, Vol. 2, Editors, Alan S. Gurman and David P. Kniskan. New York: Brunner/Mazel, 1991.

Friedman, E. Generation to Generation. New York: Guliford Press, 1986.

Geisel, T. S. & Geisel, T. S. Green Eggs and Hham. New York: Random House, 1960.

Gleick, J. CHAOS: Making a New Science. New York: Penguin Books, 1987.

Grant, T. The Silence of Unknowing. Liguori, MO: Triumph Books, 1995.

Hesselbein, Frances & Goldsmith. Marshall editors. Leaders of the Future 2. San Francisco: Jossey-Bass, 2006.

Isaacs, W. N. Dialogue and the Art of Thinking Together. New York: Doubleday, 1999.

Isaacs, W. N. *Taking Flight: Dialogue, Collective Thinking and Organizational Learning.* Organizational Dynamics, 22, 24-40, 1993.

Johnson, B. Polarity Management: Identifying and Managing Unsolvable Problems. Amherst, MA: HRD Press, 1992.

Mezirow, J. Transformative Dimensions of Adult Learning. San Francisco: Jossey-Bass, 1991.

Nouwen, H. The Way of the Heart. San Francisco: Harper San Francisco, 1981.

Nouwen, H. Reaching Out. New York: Image, 1975.

Papero, D. V. Bowen Family Systems Theory. Allyn & Bacon, 1990.

Pearls, F. Gestalt Therapy Verbatim. Moab, Utah: Real People Press, 1969.

Peck, M. S. The Different Drum. New York: Touchstone, 1987.

Robinson, G. Unpublished personal journal, 1993.

Robinson, G. & Rose, M. A Leadership Paradox: Influencing Others by Defining Yourself – Revised Edition. Indiana: AuthorHouse, 2006.

Schon, D. The Reflective Practitioner. New York: Basic Books, 1990.

Senge, P. The Fifth Discipline. New York: Currency Doubleday, 1990.

Senge, P, Kleiner, A., Roberts, C., Ross, R. & Smith, B. The Fifth Discipline Fieldbook. New York: Currency Doubleday, 1994.

Steinke, P. How Your Church Family Works. New York: Alban Institute, 1993.

Voyer, J.J. Gould, J.M. & Ford, D.N. *Systematic creation of organizational anxiety*, The Journal of Applied Behavioral Psychology, Nov-December, pp.471-89, 1997.

Wheatley, M. J. Leadership and the New Science. San Francisco: Berrett-Koehler Publishers, Inc., 1992.

Wheatley, M. J. & Kellnor-Rogers, M. *Bringing Life to Organizational Change*, Journal of Strategic Performance Measurement, April/May, pp. 5-13, 1998.

About the Authors

GREG ROBINSON is currently President of Challenge Quest, LLC in Pryor, Oklahoma. Previous to coming to Challenge Quest, Greg spent 5 years with Williams in Tulsa, Oklahoma as a Managing Organization Development Consultant. He also was the coordinator of experiential training at John Brown University.

Greg has a Ph.D. in Organizational Behavior and Leadership from The Union Institute and University in Cincinnati, Ohio. He also has a M.S. in Counseling from John Brown University.

Greg's professional career has concentrated in the areas of team development, leadership development, facilitation and consulting with organizational change efforts. He is the author of Teams for a New Generation: An Introduction to Collective Learning and A Leadership Paradox: Influencing Others by Defining Yourself.

Greg currently resides with his wife Jeannie, his daughter Keely and son Kobe in Pryor, Oklahoma.

Greg@challengequest.com

www.Challengequest.com

Mark Rose is a senior consultant with Challenge Quest, LLC and owner of MG Rose Enterprises, Inc. He works in a variety of areas for Challenge Quest including business development. Prior to working with Challenge Quest, Mark was the Program Manager for Executive Training ~ Team Quest with The University of Oklahoma. His main focus is equipping teams with skills and tools to become more effective. He received his B.A. in Public Relations and his Master's of Human Relations degree from The University of Oklahoma.

Mark has worked as co-facilitator in a series of training videos, Trainer Games in Action: Volume One and Two. These two videos show how trainers can use games and activities as object lessons in a training room to help the learner with the retention of information. Both videos have received the 2003 American Society for Training and Development's Award of Excellence. Another product Mark helped design and develop is a training tool called Expression Cards.

Mark is a certified challenge course instructor who has worked in the experiential learning field with clients in non-profit companies, government agencies and corporations. He is a skilled facilitator, and excels in his ability to enable clients to relate challenge course behaviors to actual work and home behaviors. He has co-authored a book called A Leadership Paradox: Influencing Others by Defining Yourself-Revised Edition. This book explores the leader's role in the process of profound and sustainable change in organizations.

Mark completed his Certificate of Achievement from the OU Training & Development Certificate Program in December 1999 and now teaches in the program. He is a former ASTD Executive Board member and also a member of several national organizations including the Association for Experiential Education and the Association for Challenge Course Technology.

Mark@challengequest.com

www.Challengequest.com

CPSIA information can be obtained
at www.ICGtesting.com
Printed in the USA
LVHW061003160223
739665LV00011B/276